HOMEMADE
PRESERVES

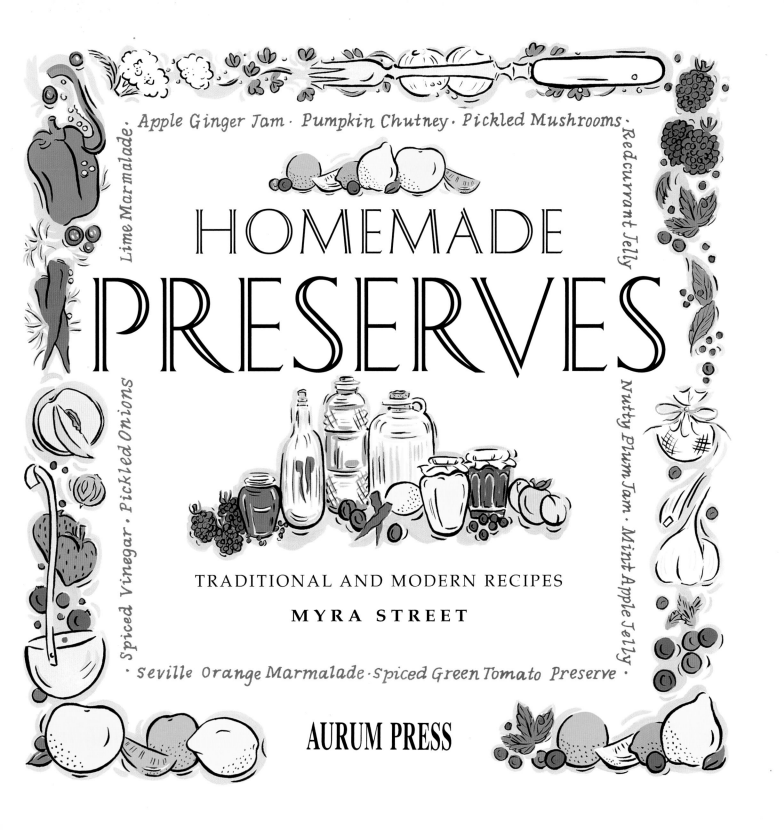

Apple Ginger Jam · Pumpkin Chutney · Pickled Mushrooms

Lime Marmalade

Redcurrant Jelly

HOMEMADE
PRESERVES

Spiced Vinegar · Pickled Onions

Nutty Plum Jam · Mint Apple Jelly

TRADITIONAL AND MODERN RECIPES

MYRA STREET

· Seville Orange Marmalade · Spiced Green Tomato Preserve ·

AURUM PRESS

A QUINTET BOOK

First published 1996 by Aurum Press Limited
25 Bedford Avenue
London WC1B 3AT
Copyright © 1996 by
Quintet Publishing Limited

A catalogue record for this book is available
from the British Library.

ISBN 1-85410-396-2

This book was designed and produced
by Quintet Publishing Limited
6 Blundell Street
London N7 9BH

Creative Director: Richard Dewing
Designer: Ian Hunt
Senior Editor: Laura Sandelson
Editor: Caroline Ball
Illustrator: Joanne Makin

Typeset in Great Britain by
Central Southern Typesetters, Eastbourne
Manufactured in Singapore by
Eray Scan (Pte) Ltd.
Printed in Singapore by
Star Standard Industries (Pte) Ltd.

Contents

Introduction

~

THE WIDE SCOPE of preserving foods in season stretches way beyond the cosy picture of the farmhouse dresser and the artistically labelled jars of jam and pickles. Centuries of skill in preserving food before the advent of freezing has given us a wonderful heritage to draw from. In this busy and high-tech age it is interesting to see that although commercially prepared jams, jellies and pickles are of a reasonable standard they are rarely in the same class as the homemade variety.

The main objective of food preservation is to use the food at maximum palatability and nutritive value before the natural decaying process begins. Most people who are interested in preserving food have freezers and refrigerators and this is now the main way of storing food in good condition. Indeed, the freezer can be an invaluable aid to making home-made preserves as the fruit can be stored in the freezer until time is available to prepare and cook it. In this way home preserves can be made in small batches as so many people work outside the home and are unable to spend hours over the stove when the fruit is just ripe or Seville oranges are in season.

We now have the advantage of buying many fruits and vegetables out of season as they are brought in from all parts of the world. This type of produce is usually expensive and it is still better to preserve fruit and vegetables in season for flavour and quality. Raspberries, strawberries, plums, cherries and blackberries all make delicious jams but the end product would be too expensive if imported fruit were used.

Although the cost of ingredients and fuel has now increased it is still possible to save money and eat delicious home preserves if you are willing to take the time. People with compact kitchens and little storage space can make small quantities and will find the microwave oven useful for keeping up a supply of homemade jam or marmalade.

Many people are experimenting with home preserving for the first time, not only to obtain excellent flavours but to ensure the ingredients are fresh, wholesome and free from artificial preservatives.

Homemade jams, jellies, and marmalades should be eaten within a year for maximum flavour, because chemical substances called enzymes are naturally introduced into the food during the home preservation process it will eventually break down and produce moulds and bacteria which will cause the food to deteriorate. This is why you may have had to scrape the mould from a precious jar of jam. This usually means that it has been kept too long, been badly sealed or stored in a damp place. It is quite safe to eat jam when mould has been removed. All homemade preserves should be rotated and eaten before the fruits and vegetables come into season the next year. If you have made too many jars, use them as presents.

Equipment for simple home preserving is minimal, and although a large preserving pan is useful if you intend to make jams and marmalade several times a year, a large, thick-bottomed, everyday saucepan can be used. Glass storage jars must be thoroughly washed and sterilized to prevent spoilage of jams, jellies, pickles and chutneys. Fill the jars right to the top and cover with waxed discs while still hot.

Making flavoured oils and vinegars is also simple and effective and can add extra taste to salad dressings as well as to cooking meats, vegetables and fish.

The range of your store cupboard will be extended with a selection of the preserves from this book. Jams and jellies are ready for delicious tea-times, tangy marmalades for breakfast, curds for cake and pudding fillings, interesting chutneys and pickles will cheer up a snack lunch or a light meal.

CHAPTER ONE

Jams for
every season

PRESERVING FRUIT IN jam is one of the more satisfying cookery tasks as the finished products are pretty colourful jars of jam to enjoy throughout the year, unlike a cake or pudding which is quickly eaten.

Making jams, jellies and marmalades is still the most popular form of fruit preservation today. Once you have tasted really good homemade preserves, you will always want to eat them. People who grow fruit in the garden often have too much to eat at one time and even to store in the freezer, therefore the surplus is ideal for jam. Those of us who do not have gardens capable of growing fruit can also make jam if we keep an eye on prices when the soft fruits are in season. There is usually a time when prices in the shops are low enough to make jam viable. There are also now many pick your own fruit farms and these are well worth a day out with the family or friends to make sure that you have a supply of jam for the rest of the year. Do take your own containers as the fruit growers often charge a great deal for them.

What makes a good jam?

All jams and marmalades are preserves of cooked fruit boiled with sugar until setting point is reached. A well-made jam has a bright colour with the full flavour of the fruit and should set or gel without becoming too stiff. In some jams, such as strawberry and cherry, the colour and flavour are more important than the set.

The keeping qualities of jam depend on the proportion of sugar to fruit, and jam must contain at least 65% sugar if it is to be kept for any length of time. Sugar is therefore a very important preserving agent in jams, jellies and marmalades, it has an influence on the flavour and reacts with the pectin and acid to obtain a good set.

A good jam, jelly or marmalade should be well set without being stiff. The end product should have a good flavour, a clear bright colour and good keeping qualities. Jams and marmalades should keep in good condition for well over one year. It is best to use up jam at this stage and make new jam with the next year's fruits. Some colour and flavour will be lost and the jam may dry up if it is keep too long even under the best storage conditions.

EQUIPMENT FOR JAM-MAKING

A PRESERVING PAN is useful if you intend to make jams or chutneys regularly; otherwise use a very large saucepan with a thick bottom. Old copper and brass preserving pans are best kept for decoration as they react with the vitamin C in the fruit. If used, they must be scrupulously clean as verdigris can form in these old pans. Modern pans are usually made of aluminium or stainless steel.

It is best to cook hard fruit in a saucepan with a lid before making jam as the wide preserving pan allows too much evaporation.

Rub butter round the preserving pan before making jam as this prevents sticking and reduces scum.

A WOODEN SPOON is needed with a handle long enough to ensure it does not fall into the large pan.

JARS should only be used if they are undamaged. Wash thoroughly with detergent and then rinse several times with hot water. Do not dry with a cloth but shake out excess water and dry in the oven.

JAM POT COVERS should be waxed discs to fit the jars, with cellophane tops which are fastened by rubber bands. Parchment tops will need thin string tied around the jar. Once the jam is covered with a waxed disc, the jar can then be covered with a clean cloth or piece of greaseproof paper until the jam is cool. The jars can then be covered with stretched film. Do not use metal screw tops as the jam will go mouldy.

A WIDE-NECKED PLASTIC FUNNEL saves messy jar filling. Place the funnel in the jar and scoop out the jam with a ladle or jug. Use a saucer under the jug to avoid spillage.

A SUGAR THERMOMETER is not essential but is a great help if you intend making lots of jams and marmalades. How to use is discussed in testing jam (see page 10).

LABELS should be written with the type of jam and the date the jam was made. Wipe the filled jars and label before storing.

Although this is a rewarding craft, there are several facts to remember and a few rules which must be followed to ensure perfect results for each batch.

SETTING JAMS AND JELLIES

The set, which allows the jam to be spread, is dependent on a gum-like substance called pectin which is found in the fruit. The pectin reacts with the acid and sugar to form a gel.

In ripe fruit the pectin is soluble and can be set free easily by stewing or crushing the fruit for a short time. Under-ripe fruit has an insoluble form of pectin known as pectose (also present in citrus fruits which explains the long cooking when making marmalade) and this can be converted to pectin by stewing with acid (lemon juice or tartaric acid). Over-ripe fruit contains pectic acid which is useless for jam making, so **do not use over-ripe fruit to make jam.**

GUIDE TO THE PECTIN CONTENT OF FRUITS USED FOR JAM AND JELLY MAKING		
HIGH	**MEDIUM**	**LOW**
CRAB APPLES	DESSERT APPLES	BANANAS
CRANBERRIES	APRICOTS	CHERRIES
COOKING APPLES	BLACKBERRIES	FIGS
BLACKCURRANTS	GREENGAGES	GRAPES
ELDERBERRIES	LOGANBERRIES	JAPONICA
REDCURRANTS	MULBERRIES	MARROWS
DAMSONS	PLUMS	MEDLARS
GOOSEBERRIES	RASPBERRIES	MELONS
LEMONS		NECTARINES
LIMES		PEACHES
SEVILLE ORANGES		PINEAPPLE
QUINCES		STRAWBERRIES
PLUMS (SOME)		RHUBARB

Of the three ingredients needed to form a gel, sugar is the only one that can be added in exact quantities. The amount of the other two depends on the state of the fruit.

Acid is often added in the form of lemon juice as it helps the pectin to form a gel, prevents crystals of sugar from forming during storage and improves the colour and flavour of the jam.

Fruits contain different amounts of pectin and some make the jam-making process simple as they are high in the substance. Often two fruits, such as blackberry and apple, are combined to make a pectin-strong mixture.

Fruit with a high pectin content requires some water in the cooking process to prevent the jam from becoming too stiff.

Only a small amount of water is added to the hard fruits in the Medium column to soften them and free the pectin, and this will be boiled away before the addition of sugar.

No water is added to the Low group but acid (lemon juice or tartaric acid) is added, as well as some other fruit which is high in pectin, such as cooking apples or redcurrants.

Adding acid

It is essential to add acid to low-pectin fruits to produce a gel. Add 2 tbsp lemon juice or ½–1 level tsp tartaric acid (available from chemists) to each 1 kg/2¼ lb fruit. Add the acid to the fruit before cooking except if using dried fruit.

A fruit with little pectin can be combined with one with a high pectin content for a better flavour and set. Redcurrant, gooseberry juice and apples are often used in this way e.g.
- strawberry with redcurrant
- cherry with redcurrant or gooseberry
- blackberry and apple
- pear and apple

Commercially prepared pectin

This can be bought in the chemist for use with low pectin fruit. If using, follow the instructions carefully. The combination fruits will work equally well.

SUGAR IN JAM MAKING

Sugar is an important ingredient in jam making as it is the substance which preserves the fruit and gives it a good keeping quality. Too much or too little sugar will result in a poor set and the flavouring of the jam will be spoiled by too much sugar.

Home-made jams which combine the best combinations of keeping qualities, a good set and excellent flavour and colour are obtained when 60% of the final weight of the jam is provided by the added sugar. For each 2.8 kg/6 lb sugar a yield of about 4.5 kg/10 lb jam is possible.

Suitable sugar for jams and jellies

Both cane and beet sugar are suitable for preserving.

GRANULATED SUGAR is the cheapest and most widely used sugar. It is suited to preserving provided it is given sufficient time to dissolve completely. Many people make excellent preserves with it.

GOLDEN GRANULATED SUGAR is a natural beet sugar which is suitable for jams and jellies.

PRESERVING SUGAR is a sugar with large crystals ideally suited to making jams and jellies. The crystals dissolve slowly and retain enough space between them to prevent the sugar settling in a dense layer at the bottom of the pan. This prevents any sticking and the jam requires less attention. Preserving sugar produces less froth and scum, which means the preserves require less skimming and the jam should be brighter.

JAM SUGAR is a special sugar for making jam and is especially suitable for use with low-pectin fruit such as strawberries and cherries. It is excellent for beginners making a small quantity of jam but it is more expensive for large quantities.

LIGHT BROWN MUSCOVADO can be used in some marmalades and jams to give a rich dark colour. It is also useful in chutneys.

DARK BROWN MUSCOVADO is suitable for chutneys and pickles.

DARK BROWN SOFT CANE SUGAR is also suitable for chutneys and pickles.

MOLASSES SUGAR contains the highest amount of natural molasses and is almost black in colour. Use in recipes which call for dark brown sugar such as Christmas cakes, mincemeat and some chutneys and pickles.

DEMERARA SUGAR has large sparkling crystals with a crunchy, sticky texture and a rich aroma. It is used for coffee and crumb toppings on cakes and puddings and only used in preserving in special recipes.

CASTER SUGAR is light and has a fine grain, it is more expensive than granulated and is only used in preserving in special recipes.

In most recipes it is suggested that the sugar is warmed. This is not essential but it does help the sugar to dissolve more quickly when added to the hot fruit. Heat the sugar in the oven with the jam jars, making sure that it is in a heatproof container. The sugar is then dissolved over a low heat, stirring from time to time.

Sugar has a hardening effect on fruits such as blackcurrants and damsons, therefore it is essential to soften the fruit thoroughly before adding the sugar.

TESTING THE JAM FOR SETTING

Although it is quite easy to make jams and jellies with simple household tests, anyone who makes a great deal of jam or marmalade will find that investing in a sugar thermometer is the best way to test for setting.

To use a sugar thermometer for jam, it should first be put into hot water. Stir the jam thoroughly before the temperature is tested and take the thermometer straight from the hot water to the hot jam. The bulb of the thermometer should not rest on the bottom of the pan. The temperature for jam or jelly should be about 105°C/220°F. At the same time it is useful to do the cold plate test.

Cold plate test
Put a plate in the freezer or freezing compartment of the refrigerator for five minutes. Place a scant teaspoon of the jam on the plate. If the jam has reached setting point the surface should set and become crinkly. Use only a small amount of jam or it will not cool down quickly enough to give a true test.

The flake test
Dip a wooden spoon into the jam and turn it horizontally in the hand until the jam on it is slightly cooled. The jam will run off the edge in large flakes instead of droplets if the jam is set.

POTTING AND STORING JAM

Clean glass jars can be placed on newspapers on the oven shelves in a low oven ready for the jam. Remove any scum from the jam at this stage; constant skimming during cooking is not necessary and will reduce the yield. Lift the hot jars onto a heatproof surface and have the preserving pan beside them. Pour the hot jam into the pots using a jug or ladle, preferably through a wide plastic funnel stuck in the mouth of the jar (this will stop any drips).

Sparkling Strawberry Jam

The favourite summer fruits do make the most delicious jams. A scone with cream and home-made jam, especially strawberry or raspberry, makes tea-time into a banquet. You may have to find a hiding place for your jam if you have a family as it can disappear quite rapidly. Beware of over-boiling these delicate jams as the colour and texture can be impaired.

MAKES 4.5 KG/10 LB

3.2 kg/7 lb strawberries, hulled
juice of 2 lemons
2.8 kg/6 lb sugar, warmed

Wash the strawberries if necessary and pat dry with some kitchen paper. Put in the preserving pan with the lemon juice and stir gently over a low heat to produce some juice and reduce the volume of the fruit.

Add the sugar and stir over a low heat from time to time until the sugar is completely dissolved. Bring the jam to a rolling boil for a few minutes, then test for setting or allow the sugar thermometer to reach 105°C/220°F.

Remove any scum which has formed and allow the jam to cool until a skin is just forming. This will make sure that the fruit does not float to the top of the jars. Pour into hot jars, seal, cover and label.

Microwave Strawberry Jam

MAKES ABOUT 1.4 KG/3 LB

900 g/2 lb strawberries, hulled
3 tbsp lemon juice
1 kg/2¼ lb sugar

Rinse the strawberries and pat dry with kitchen paper. Put into a large (3.5-ltr/6-pt) bowl suitable for the microwave.

Add the sugar, mix well, microwave on full power for 5 minutes. Remove and stir well to dissolve the sugar.

Return to the microwave oven and cook for 10–12 minutes on full power, stirring twice during the cooking time. Remove from the oven, skim off any scum and test for setting.

Allow to stand for a few minutes. Pour into hot jars, seal, cover and label.

Freezer Jam

This is more a conserve than a jam and it can be served semi-frozen. Raspberries, strawberries, peaches and nectarines are all suitable. For peaches and nectarines there is no need to skin, just stone and mince in the food processor or chop finely with a knife.

MAKES ABOUT 900 G/2 LB

450 g/1 lb fresh soft fruit
450 g/1 lb sugar
2 tbsp lemon juice

Place the prepared fruit in a large bowl with the sugar and the lemon juice. Stir and leave in a warm place for several hours or until the fruit has softened and the sugar dissolved.

Pour into small plastic containers and freeze with a dated label. The jam can be frozen for 9 months but once opened it can only be stored in the fridge for 3 weeks.

The jam will need about 15–20 minutes to defrost.

Dazzling Raspberry Jam

This is one of the most delicious and favourite jams; it should be a brilliant jewel colour with a fresh flavour. It is best made with fruit which is just ripe. As it is important to gauge the boiling temperature, it is made more accurately with a sugar thermometer.

MAKES 3.2 KG/7 LB

1.8 kg/4 lb raspberries
2 tbsp lemon juice
1.8 kg/4 lb sugar, warmed

Heat the washed fruit and lemon juice gently in the pan until the juice starts to flow. Add the sugar and stir from time to time over a low heat until completely dissolved. Bring to a rolling boil and test after 3 minutes or using the sugar thermometer when the temperature reaches 105°C/220°F. Try not to overboil as the flavour and colour will spoil.

Pour into hot jars, seal, cover and label.

Microwave Raspberry Jam

MAKES 1.4 KG/3 LB

900 g/2 lb raspberries
3 tbsp lemon juice
1 kg/2¼ lb sugar

If using frozen raspberries, defrost them for about 8 minutes, or cook for 3 minutes if using fresh. Add the lemon juice and allow the fruit to cook for a further 2 minutes.

Stir in the sugar and cook at full power for 4 minutes, remove from the oven and stir.

Cook at full power for about 15–20 minutes, but stir after 10 minutes and again after a further 5 minutes. Test for setting, but this jam always sets well after cooling so do not be too alarmed if it seems a little runny.

Allow to cool slightly as it is very hot to handle. Pour into hot jars, seal, cover and label.

Speedy Microwave Raspberry Jam

MAKES 700 G/1½ LB

450 g/1 lb frozen raspberries
2 tbsp lemon juice
450 g/1 lb granulated or preserving sugar

Put the raspberries in a large bowl suitable for the microwave oven. Allow to defrost for 3 minutes and cook for 2 minutes on full power.

Add lemon juice, stir in the sugar and cook at full power for 4 minutes and stir thoroughly. Cook for a further 15 minutes, remove any scum and allow to stand for 3 minutes.

Pour into hot jars, seal, cover and label.

Uncooked Raspberry Jam

MAKES 900 G/2 LB

450 g/1 lb raspberries
550 g/1¼ lb sugar

The raspberries must be firm, ripe and dry or the jam will not keep. To clean, roll gently in paper kitchen towel. Put in a bowl with the sugar and beat well until the sugar is completely dissolved; this can take 30–40 minutes. Alternatively, use a food mixer or a food processor for a shorter preparation time. When the sugar is dissolved, pour into pots, cover and store in the refrigerator, or the freezer if keeping for any time. Eat within two weeks.

Ruby Rhubarb and Raspberry Jam

MAKES ABOUT 1.5 KG/3½ LB

700 g/1½ lb rhubarb
300 g/11 oz raspberries (frozen can be used)
juice of 1 lemon
1 kg/2¼ lb sugar, warmed

Wash the rhubarb and raspberries. Cut the rhubarb into small pieces. Put both fruits with the lemon juice into a large pan and stir over a low heat until juice starts to run from the raspberries. Allow to simmer for a few minutes (do not burn) and then add the sugar.

Continue cooking over a low heat, stirring from time to time until the sugar is dissolved and the rhubarb is soft.

Bring to a rolling boil for about 4 minutes and then test for setting or use the sugar thermometer until it reads 105°C/220°F.

Pour into hot jars, seal, cover and label.

Jewelled Raspberry and Redcurrant Jam

The combination of redcurrants and raspberries gives the jam a superb flavour and a brilliant colour.

MAKES ABOUT 4.5 KG/10 LB

600 ml/1 pt redcurrant juice (see below)
1.8 kg/4 lb raspberries
2.8 kg/6 lb preserving sugar, warmed
2 tbsp lemon juice

Make the redcurrant juice by stewing 1 kg/2¼ lb redcurrants in the microwave until soft (about 10 minutes) or in a saucepan with 1 tbsp water. When soft, liquidize and put through a nylon sieve.

Put the raspberries into a pan and allow them to warm over a low heat. When the juice starts to run add the redcurrant juice, lemon juice and stir gently. Allow the fruit to simmer gently for about 20 minutes.

Add the warmed sugar and stir until it is completely dissolved. Bring the jam to a rolling boil and after 3–5 minutes test for setting or use the sugar thermometer until it reaches 105°C/220°F.

Pour into hot jars, seal, cover and label.

Raspberry and Apple Jam

MAKES 4 KG/8–9 LB

1 kg/2¼ lb cooking apples, peeled, cored and sliced
juice of 2 lemons
150 ml/¼ pt water
1 kg/2¼ lb raspberries, hulled, washed and drained
1.8 kg/4 lb preserving sugar, warmed

Place the apples in a pan, mix and stir in the sugar with the lemon juice and water. Simmer until tender for about 15 minutes.

Add the raspberries and sprinkle on the warmed sugar, simmer gently until the sugar is completely dissolved. Bring to the boil for about 5 minutes. Test for setting or use the sugar thermometer to 105°C/220°F.

Allow to stand for 2–3 minutes, remove any scum and pour into hot jars, seal, cover and label.

Cherry and Redcurrant Jam

MAKES 4.5 KG/10 LB

300 ml/½ pt redcurrant juice (see below)
2.8 kg/6 lb morello cherries
2.8 kg/6 lb sugar, warmed

You will need about 700 g/1½ lb redcurrants to make the juice. Put the washed currants in the microwave for 8 minutes until the juice runs or in a small saucepan over a very low heat. Mash the fruit with a potato masher or put through a liquidizer or food processor. Rub through a coarse sieve until you have 300 ml/½ pt of juice.

Remove the stones from the cherries, preferably with a cherry stoner, over a bowl to catch the juice. If you prefer, put them in a pan with 150 ml/¼ pt water and stew for about 10 minutes until soft, then turn the cherries into a bowl. Allow to cool, then remove the stones. Crack about 20 cherry stones, remove the kernels and tie into a muslin bag.

Put the redcurrant juice into the preserving pan with the sugar and allow the sugar to dissolve over a low heat.

When the sugar is completely dissolved, add the cherries and bring to a rolling boil for about 10–15 minutes. Test for setting or use the sugar thermometer which should reach 105°C/220°F.

Pour into hot jars, seal, cover and label.

Luscious Cherry Jam

Cherries have practically no pectin, therefore it is a more difficult jam to make. It is possible to obtain a good set by using a high proportion of sugar to fruit. Cut the acid in half if using morello cherries. The black sweet cherries are more suitable for bottling or freezing.

MAKES ABOUT 5.5 KG/12 LB

4.5 kg/10 lb cherries, weight after removing stones
juice of 5 lemons or 15 g/½ oz citric or tartaric acid
3.2 kg/7 lb sugar, warmed

After stoning the cherries with a stoner, place the stones on a square of muslin with the peel of at least one lemon, cut up. Tie the muslin into a bag and place in the preserving pan with the cherries, lemon juice and 150 ml/¼ pt water. Heat slowly over a low heat until the juice runs, then simmer the pan until the cherries are tender, which will take about 30 minutes.

Add the warmed sugar and stir until completely dissolved. Bring the pan to a rolling boil until the jam reaches setting point or the sugar thermometer reaches 105°C/220°F. Allow to stand for a few minutes and remove any scum from the surface.

Pour into hot jars, seal, cover and label.

Fragrant Rose Petal Jam

MAKES ABOUT 1.1 KG/2½ LB

450 g/1 lb rose petals
450 g/1 lb lemons
450 g/1 lb sugar, warmed

Trim off the white tips of the rose petals. Slice the lemons very thinly with a sharp knife and put in a saucepan just covered with water. Bring to the boil and drain, retaining the liquid.

Add the sugar to the lemons and stir until dissolved with 2 tbsp of the drained liquid. Stir in the rose petals and cook until the mixture is thick. Pour into hot jars, seal, cover and label.

Blackcurrant Jam

Blackcurrants are sometimes scarce now unless you grow your own. Most of the crops go to the soft drink manufacturers so look out for them in the summer.

MAKES 2.3 KG/5 LB

1 kg/2¼ lb blackcurrants
900 ml/1½ pt water
1.4 kg/3 lb sugar, warmed

Top and tail the blackcurrants and wash in a colander. Put them into a medium-sized pot, cover with the measured water and cover with a lid. A good depth of fruit and water is necessary to avoid too much moisture loss.

Stew the blackcurrants until the skins are very soft. This may take 20–30 minutes, but do make sure they are tender. Transfer into a preserving or larger pan. Add the warmed sugar and stir until it is completely dissolved. Bring the blackcurrants to a rolling boil and test for setting after about 10–15 minutes or the sugar thermometer reaches 105°C/220°F.

Pour into hot jars, seal, cover and label.

Reine Claude's Breakfast Jam

In France greengage plums are called Reine Claude's plums because they were a favourite of hers.

MAKES 2.3 KG/5 LB

1.5 kg/3 lb greengages, halved and stoned
300 ml/½ pt water
2 tbsp lemon juice
1.4 kg/3 lb sugar, warmed

Crack some of the stones and remove the kernels. Place them on a square of muslin and tie into a bag. Put the fruit with the water and lemon juice in a large saucepan and stew until tender but not mushed. You will need another 300 ml/½ pt water if the fruit is under-ripe.

Turn into the preserving pan, remove the muslin bag and squeeze to make sure all the juice goes into the jam.

Add the sugar, stir well over a low heat, then allow to dissolve slowly, stirring from time to time. When the sugar is dissolved, bring the pan to the boil and stir from time to time to prevent sticking. Boil for 5 minutes and test for setting or wait until the sugar thermometer reaches 105°C/220°F.

Pour into hot jars, seal, cover and label.

Damson Jam

MAKES 2.3 KG/5 LB

2 kg/4½ lb damsons, washed and stoned
600 ml/1 pt water
2.3 kg/5 lb sugar, warmed

Put the damsons in a large ovenproof casserole, pour on the water and cover with a tight lid. Place in an oven preheated to 150°C/300°F/Gas Mark 2 for several hours or until the fruit is tender and the juice has run out. This step can also be done in a microwave oven by putting a bowl in at full power for 15 minutes; stir and allow to stand for 5 minutes. Repeat this operation three times.

Remove damsons from the oven and measure the fruit and liquid into the preserving pan. Add an equal quantity of sugar.

Dissolve the sugar, stirring from time to time over a low heat. Bring to a rolling boil for 2–3 minutes, test for setting or use the sugar thermometer until it reaches 105°C/220°F.

Remove any scum from the jam, pour into hot jars, seal, cover and label.

Cherry and Gooseberry Jam

MAKES ABOUT 3 KG/6–7 LB

1 kg/2¼ lb sour or morello cherries, stoned
1 kg/2¼ lb gooseberries, topped and tailed
juice of 3 lemons
2 kg/4½ lb sugar, warmed

Stone the cherries carefully over a bowl to make sure all the juice is saved. Tie the stones in a square of muslin to make a bag.

Put the cherries, gooseberries, strained lemon juice and muslin bag into the preserving pan and simmer for about 20–30 minutes or until the fruit is tender. Remove the bag with the kernels.

Add the warmed sugar and allow to dissolve over a low heat stirring from time to time. Bring to the boil and keep up a rapid boil for about 15 minutes. Test for setting or until the sugar thermometer reaches 105°C/220°F.

Pour into hot jars, seal, cover and label.

Green Gooseberry Jam

MAKES 2.5 KG/5–6 LB

1.25 kg/2½ lb gooseberries, washed
600 ml/1 pt water
1.5 kg/3¼ lb sugar, warmed

Top and tail the gooseberries; cut in half to help the juice to flow more quickly. Put in a medium-sized deep saucepan with the water, making sure there is about 7–8 cm/3 in depth with the fruit and water together. This will ensure that the water does not dry out (as it would in a flat preserving pan) before the skins are tender. Stew gently for about 40 minutes.

Tip the stewed fruit into the preserving pan and add the sugar. Stir from time to time over a low heat until all the sugar is dissolved.

If the jam looks a very pale colour you can add, very carefully, about two drops of green vegetable colouring at this stage. Mix well and bring the pan to a rolling boil for a few minutes. Test for setting or allow the sugar thermometer to reach 105°C/220°F.

Pour into hot jars, seal, cover and label.

Ripe Gooseberry Jam

MAKES 1 KG/2¼ LB

1 kg/2¼ lb ripe gooseberries
1 kg/2¼ lb sugar, warmed
½ tsp Angostura Bitters

Clean the ripe gooseberries, discarding any that are damaged. Chop them roughly with a sharp knife or put into the food processor or liquidizer until roughly chopped.

Put the fruit with the sugar into a large saucepan or preserving pan and mix well. Cook over a low heat until the sugar is completely dissolved, stirring from time to time.

Bring the pan to a full rolling boil and continue for about 4 minutes before testing for setting or use the sugar thermometer until it reaches 105°C/ 225°F. Add the Angostura Bitters, if using, and stir round.

Pour immediately into hot jars, seal, cover and label.

Plum Jam

MAKES 2.5 KG/5–6 LB

1.5 kg/3 lb plums, washed,
halved and stoned
4 tbsp lemon juice
300 ml/¹⁄₂ pt water
1.4 kg/3 lb sugar, warmed

Crack about half the plum stones, remove the kernels and put into a muslin bag. The plums can be cut into smaller pieces, as liked.

Put the plums and lemon juice with the muslin bag in the pan with the water and bring to the boil. Lower the heat and simmer the fruit until it is tender but not mushy.

Add the sugar and allow it to dissolve over a low heat stirring from time to time.

Bring to a rolling boil for about 10 minutes and test for setting or allow the sugar thermometer to reach 105°C/220°F.

Allow to stand for 5 minutes and pour into hot jars, seal, cover and label.

Nutty Plum Jam

MAKES ABOUT 2.3 KG/5 LB

1.8 kg/4 lb plums
300 ml/¹⁄₂ pt water
1.4 kg/3 lb golden granulated sugar,
warmed
100 g/4 oz walnuts, chopped
4 tbsp brandy

Cut the plums in half, take out the stones and place them in a small pan. Pour the water over the stones and boil for 10 minutes. Strain liquid into the preserving pan. Add the plums and simmer for 10 minutes until soft, stirring frequently.

Add the warmed sugar and stir until completely dissolved. Boil rapidly for approximately 15 minutes until setting point is reached or the sugar thermometer reaches 105°C/220°F.

Remove pan from heat and add walnuts and brandy. Leave to stand for 6 minutes and stir well.

Pour into hot jars, seal, cover and label.

Green Plum Jam

This is an excellent way of using unripe plums.

MAKES ABOUT 3.5 KG/8 LB

1.8 kg/4 lb unripe plums
900 ml/1¹⁄₂ pt water
2 kg/4¹⁄₂ lb sugar, warmed

Cut the plums in half and remove the stones. Crack about half the stones and remove the kernels.

Put the sugar and water into the preserving pan and bring slowly to the boil. Lower the heat and stir over a low heat until the sugar is dissolved. Boil the dissolved sugar and water for about 15 minutes, making sure it does not burn.

Add the fruit and kernels, continue boiling until the jam is setting or until the sugar thermometer reaches 105°C/220°F.

Pour into hot jars, seal, cover and label.

Plum and Elderberry Jam

MAKES ABOUT 3 KG/6–7 LB

1 kg/2¼ lb elderberries, stalks removed
300 ml/½ pt water
1.2 kg/2½ lb plums, stoned
2 kg/4½ lb sugar, warmed

Put the prepared elderberries in a pan with 150 ml/¼ pt of the water. Bring the pan to the boil and simmer for about 5 minutes. Allow to cool and turn into a jelly bag or strain through a muslin-lined sieve overnight.

Cook the plums with the remainder of the water until tender, then add the elderberry juice. Bring to simmering point, then add the sugar over a low heat and stir until dissolved.

Bring back to the boil and allow to boil for 5 minutes. Test for setting or until the sugar thermometer reaches 105°C/220°F.

Allow to stand for a few minutes, then pour into hot jars, seal, cover and label.

Loganberry Jam

MAKES ABOUT 4.5 KG/10 LB

2.8 kg/6 lb loganberries, hulled and washed
2.8 kg/6 lb sugar, warmed

Put the fruit into the preserving pan and set over a very low heat, stirring all the time until the juice starts to run out of the fruit. Cook the fruit until it is quite soft.

Add the warmed sugar and stir over a low heat until it is completely dissolved. Raise the heat and bring the pan to a rolling boil for about 12–15 minutes. Test for setting or wait until the sugar thermometer reads 105°C/220°F.

Pour the jam into clean hot jars, seal, cover and label.

Quince Jam

MAKES 4.5 KG/10 LB

1.8 kg/4 lb quinces
1.1 ltr/2 pt water
2 lemons
2.8 kg/6 lb sugar, warmed

Peel, core and cut the quinces into cubes. Alternatively, they can be grated (this can be done in the food processor) and put into a saucepan with the water. Squeeze the lemons to remove the juice and place the lemon shells and pips from the squeezer in a muslin square, tie into a bag and add to the quinces.

Bring to the boil and simmer gently for 25 minutes until the fruit is tender.

Add the sugar and dissolve over a low heat stirring from time to time. Stir in the lemon juice and bring the pan to a rolling boil until setting point is reached or the sugar thermometer reads 105°C/220°F.

Pour into hot jars, seal, cover and label.

Fruits of Summer Jam

MAKES ABOUT 1.1 KG/2½ LB

900 g/2¼ lb strawberries, hulled and washed
225 g/8 oz redcurrants, topped and tailed
225 g/8 oz raspberries, hulled and washed
1 kg/2¼ lb golden granulated sugar

Put all the prepared fruit in a bowl and sprinkle with 2 tbsp sugar. Cover and leave overnight in the refrigerator.

Next day, tip into a large saucepan with 4 tbsp water. Simmer gently until the fruit is tender.

Add the remaining sugar and stir over a low heat until dissolved. Bring to the boil and keep on a rolling boil for 15 minutes, until setting point is reached or the sugar thermometer has reached 105°C/220°F. Remove any scum with a slotted spoon.

Allow the jam to cool for 5 minutes. Pour into hot jars, seal, cover and label.

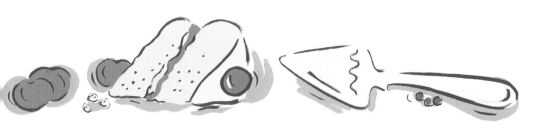

Ginger Rhubarb Jam

MAKES 2.8 KG/6 LB

1.8 kg/4 lb rhubarb, washed and trimmed
300 ml/¹/₂ pt water
4 tbsp lemon juice
5-cm/2-in piece of fresh root ginger, peeled
1.4 kg/3 lb sugar, warmed
100 g/4 oz crystallized ginger, finely chopped

Cut the rhubarb into pieces about 2–3 cm/1 in long and put into the preserving pan with the water and lemon juice. Bruise the ginger by pounding it, wrapped in film, with a weight. Add to the pan and cook over a low heat until the rhubarb is soft. Remove the ginger.

Add the sugar and stir into the mixture over a low heat until it is completely dissolved, then add the crystallized ginger and bring the pan to a rolling boil for about 10–15 minutes before testing for setting. Alternatively, cook until the sugar thermometer reaches 105°C/220°F.

Pour into hot jars, seal, cover and label.

Apricot and Rhubarb Microwave Jam

MAKES 900 G/2 LB

450 g/1 lb dried apricots
600 ml/1 pt water
450 g/1 lb rhubarb, chopped into 1 cm/¹/₂ in lengths
1 kg/2¹/₄ lb granulated or preserving sugar

Soak the apricots in the water for 24 hours if time allows. Non-soak apricots are now available but they should be soaked in the water for about 1 hour if possible. Otherwise, boil the measured water and pour over the apricots in a large bowl and cook at full power in the microwave for 3 minutes. Allow to stand for 5 minutes. In another dish cook the rhubarb in a little water for 2 minutes or until soft.

Drain the apricots, retaining the juice. Cook the apricots for a further 5 minutes. Add the rhubarb and mix well. Sprinkle on the sugar, mix well again and add the juice, made up to 600 ml/1 pt with boiling water. Cook for about 10 minutes to bring to the boil. Stir well and cook for another 10 minutes until setting point is reached or the sugar thermometer reaches 105°C/220°F. Allow to stand for 5 minutes.

Pour into the hot jars, seal, cover and label.

Rhubarb and Loganberry Jam

MAKES ABOUT 3.2 KG/7 LB

1.4 kg/3 lb red rhubarb, cut into pieces
300 ml/¹/₂ pt water
1 kg/2¹/₄ lb loganberries
2.3 kg/5 lb sugar, warmed

Use only the red parts of the rhubarb, so weigh after preparing to ensure 1.5 kg/3 lb. Put the rhubarb in the water and stew gently over a low heat, stirring from time to time, until completely tender and reduced to a pulp.

Pick over the loganberries and wash before putting into a preserving pan. Crush the fruit slightly to make the juice run. Simmer for a few minutes, pressing with a wooden spoon, then add the rhubarb and mix the two fruits over a low heat.

Tip in the sugar and mix well. Stir over a low heat from time to time until the sugar dissolves completely. Bring to a rolling boil and test for setting after about 5 minutes. Alternatively, use the sugar thermometer until it registers 105°C/220°F.

Pour into hot jars, seal, cover and label.

Tangy Rhubarb Orange Jam

MAKES ABOUT 2 KG/4½ LB

1.5 kg/3 lb rhubarb, cut into pieces
6 tbsp lemon juice
1.4 kg/3 lb sugar
3 oranges
water

Wash the rhubarb and put in a large bowl with the lemon juice and sugar. Cover with film or a clean tea-towel and allow to stand for 24 hours. Put the whole oranges in a pan, cover with water and simmer over a low heat until tender. Remove from the pan and cool, cut in half and squeeze out the juice and the pips. Cut the peel into thin slices and place in the preserving pan with the orange juice.

Add the rhubarb with the sugar and allow to dissolve over a low heat, stirring from time to time.

Bring to a rolling boil and continue boiling until setting is reached or the sugar thermometer reaches 105°C/220°F.

Pour into hot jars, then seal, cover and label.

Dried Apricot Jam

This jam is really simple to make and delicious. It can be used sieved for topping fruit flans or any dish that requires an apricot glaze.

MAKES ABOUT 2.3 KG/5 LB

450 g/1 lb dried apricots
1.75 ltr/3 pt water
2 tbsp lemon juice
1.4 kg/3 lb sugar, warmed
25 g/1 oz blanched almonds (optional)

Place the apricots in a large bowl and cover with the measured water (make sure they are completely covered). Allow to soak for 24 hours. If using the non-soak dried variety now available, leave in the water for about 1 hour. If liked, chop into pieces.

Transfer the apricots into the preserving pan with the water and simmer for about 40 minutes or until the apricots are tender. Add the lemon juice after about 20 minutes or when the fruit begins to soften.

Add the sugar and stir from time to time over a low heat until dissolved. Add the blanched almonds if using. Bring to the boil and continue to boil for 15 minutes. Test for setting, or use the sugar thermometer – 105°C/220°F. Pour into the hot jars, seal, cover and label.

Apricot Jam

MAKES 2.3 KG/5 LB

1.5 kg/3 lb apricots, halved and stoned
300 ml/½ pt water (add more if fruit is hard)
4 tbsp lemon juice
1.4 kg/3 lb sugar

Take the apricot stones and crack about half of them open to reveal the kernels. Put these in boiling water and blanch for 2–3 minutes. Wrap in a muslin square and tie like a bag.

Place the halved apricots in a large pan with the water, lemon juice and kernels. Cover the pan and stew the fruit gently over a low heat until tender. Remove the bag of kernels.

Add the warmed sugar and stir over a low heat until it is completely dissolved. Bring to the boil and keep on a rolling boil for about 15 minutes, test for setting or use the sugar thermometer to check when it reaches 105°C/220°F. Pour into the hot jars, seal, cover and label.

Apple and Apricot Jam

MAKES 2.3 KG/5 LB

*1.kg/2¼ lb fresh apricots,
halved and stoned
1 kg/2¼ lb cooking apples,
peeled and cored
600 ml/1 pt water
2 kg/4½ lb sugar, warmed*

Put the halved apricots into the preserving pan. Slice the apples and add to the pan with the water. Simmer for about 20 minutes until the fruit is tender.

Add the warmed sugar and stir from time to time until it is completely dissolved. Bring to the boil and cook for about 15 minutes until setting point is reached or the sugar thermometer reaches 105°C/220°F.

Pour into hot jars, seal, cover and label.

Pear and Apricot Jam

MAKES 3 KG/6½ LB

*450 g/1 lb dried apricots, cut in half
900 ml/1½ pt water
1.4 kg/3 lb pears, peeled and sliced
juice of 2 lemons
1.6 kg/3½ lb sugar, warmed*

Soak apricots overnight or use the non-soak variety now available. If using non-soak allow the apricots to soak in the measured water for about 1 hour. Put the drained apricots into the preserving pan with the sliced pears, lemon juice and half the strained water. Bring to the boil and then lower the heat and simmer for about 30 minutes until tender.

Add the sugar and stir from time to time over a low heat until the sugar is completely dissolved. Bring up to a rolling boil and test for setting after 5 minutes or when the sugar thermometer reaches 105°C/220°F.

Allow to stand for 5 minutes, then pour into hot jars, seal, cover and label.

Gingery Pumpkin and Apricot Jam

MAKES 2.8 KG/6 LB

*450 g/1 lb dried apricots, halved
1 kg/2¼ lb pumpkin flesh (weight after removing skin and seeds)
1.2 kg/2½ lb sugar
15 g/½ oz crystallized ginger, chopped*

Put the halved apricots in a bowl, just cover with water and allow to stand for 24 hours. Place the pumpkin flesh in another bowl and sprinkle with 800 g/1½ lb of the sugar. Allow to stand for 24 hours.

Put the apricots, with the liquid from the bowl, the pumpkin with its sugary juice and the remaining sugar in the preserving pan with the chopped ginger. Stir over a low heat until the sugar has completely dissolved. Bring to a rolling boil until the setting point is reached or the sugar thermometer reads 105°C/220°F.

Allow to stand for 5 minutes and pour into hot jars, seal, cover and label.

Apple Ginger Jam

MAKES 2.3 KG/5 LB

1.4 kg/3 lb apples
600 ml/1 pt water
grated rind of 1 orange
grated rind of 1 lemon
2 level tsp ground ginger or 25 g/1 oz
preserved ginger, chopped finely
5 tbsp lemon juice
1.4 kg/3 lb sugar, warmed

Prepare the apples by peeling, coring and slicing. Retain all the skin and core, place in a muslin square and tie into a bag.

Place the apples, water, muslin bag, rind and the ginger in a large pan and stew until the fruit is tender.

Remove the bag and add the lemon juice to the fruit before adding the sugar.

Dissolve the sugar over a low heat, stirring from time to time. Bring to a rolling boil and stir from time to time until setting stage is reached (about 15 minutes) or until the sugar thermometer reaches 105°C/220°F.

Pour into hot jars, seal, cover and label.

High Dumpsie Dearie Jam

This is an old country recipe. Make it in the autumn when garden apples and pears are plentiful.

MAKES ABOUT 2.3 KG/5 LB

450 g/1 lb cooking apples, peeled and cored
450 g/1 lb pears, peeled and cored
450 g/1 lb plums, halved and stoned
25 g/1 oz root ginger, bruised
300 ml/½ pt water
grated rind and juice of 1 lemon
about 1.4 kg/3 lb sugar

Prepare the fruits (retain the plum stones) and ginger (bruise the ginger by hitting it with a rolling pin or meat mallet). Put the fruit and ginger into the preserving pan with the water and lemon juice. If liked, put the stones and the lemon rind into a muslin square, tie into a bag and add to the pan. Bring the pan to the boil and simmer the fruit until it is tender.

Tip the stewed fruit into a large bowl or saucepan and measure back into the preserving pan. Squeeze out the muslin bag, remove the bag and the ginger. For each 600 ml/1 pt stewed fruit, allow 350 g/12 oz sugar, stir over a low heat until the sugar is dissolved.

Bring up to a rolling boil and continue to cook for about 10 minutes until setting point is reached or the sugar thermometer reaches 105°C/220°F.

Pour into hot jars, seal, cover and label.

Blackberry and Apple Jam

MAKES 4.5 KG/10 LB

1.8 kg/4 lb blackberries
300 ml/½ pt water
1.8 kg/4 lb cooking apples, peeled,
cored and sliced
2.8 kg/6 lb sugar, warmed

Place the blackberries in a large saucepan with half the water and cook gently until soft. Put the apples with the remaining water in the preserving pan and cook over a gentle heat until tender.

Tip in the cooked blackberries (they may be sieved and added as a purée if a smooth jam is preferred). Sprinkle on the warmed sugar and stir from time to time over a low heat until dissolved. Bring to the boil for about 15 minutes until set or until the sugar thermometer reaches 105°C/220°F.

Pour into the hot jars, seal, cover and label.

Autumn Pear and Apple Jam

MAKES ABOUT 3 KG/6–7 LB

1 kg/2¼ lb cooking apples,
peeled and cored
1 kg/2¼ lb pears, peeled and cored
1 small cinnamon stick
450 ml/¾ pt water
1.8 kg/4 lb sugar, warmed
finely grated rind and juice of 2 lemons

Prepare the fruit and cut into small pieces.

Put the cinnamon stick and the water in a small pan and allow to simmer for about 20 minutes.

Put the sugar in the preserving pan and strain the water from the small pan on to the sugar. Mix well and stir over a low heat until dissolved. Add the rind and the strained lemon juice, then add the apples and pears. Bring the pan to a rolling boil and continue to boil for about 15 minutes and then test for setting. If using a sugar thermometer it should reach 105°C/220°F.

Pour into hot jars, seal, cover and label.

Vanilla Pear Jam

An excellent way to use up excess dessert pears if you have a tree. Make the jam just as the pears are beginning to ripen. If you don't have a tree halve the ingredients for a smaller quantity.

MAKES ABOUT 4.5 KG/10 LB

4 kg/10 lb pears
2 level tsp tartaric acid
about 3.5 kg/8 lb sugar
1 vanilla pod

Peel and core the pears and cut into small pieces with a sharp knife or use the thick slicing blade on the food processor. Put in the preserving pan and cover with boiling water. Simmer until tender, then strain the water off into a pan or jug.

Weigh the cooked fruit and allow 450 g/1 lb of sugar to every 450 g/1 lb fruit. Put the sugar into a preserving pan and add 300 ml/½ pt pear water. Dissolve the sugar slowly over a low heat.

Add the cooked pears and the vanilla pod. Bring the pan to a rolling boil and keep boiling until the jam is golden brown and thick like marmalade. Test for setting or use the sugar thermometer until it reads 105°C/220°F.

Pour into hot jars, seal, cover and label.

Spiced Peach Jam

MAKES 2.7 KG/6 LB

1 cooking apple, sliced and
chopped with core
rind of 2 lemons, finely peeled
2 cloves
1.6 kg/3½ lb ripe peaches,
stoned and sliced
2 tbsp lemon juice, optional
300 ml/½ pt water
1 tsp allspice
1.6 kg/3½ lb sugar, warmed

Make a square with a double piece of muslin and place the apple with pips and core on the muslin with the lemon rind and the cloves; tie into a bag.

Place the peaches into the pan with the water and the muslin bag. Two tbsp of lemon juice can be added at this stage, if liked.

Bring the peaches to the boil and turn down the heat and allow the fruit to simmer until soft. Add the warmed sugar and stir over a low heat until it is completely dissolved.

Turn up the heat until the contents of the pan are boiling rapidly. Continue to boil for about 15–20 minutes, until setting point is reached or the sugar thermometer has reached 105°C/220°F.

Pour into hot jars, seal, cover and label.

Golden Pineapple-Lemon Jam

MAKES ABOUT 2.8 KG/6 LB

3 lemons
1.5 kg/3 lb fresh pineapple flesh,
cut into pieces
600 ml/1 pt water
1.4 kg/3 lb sugar, warmed

Squeeze the lemons to obtain maximum juice. Put all the pips and flesh from the squeezer into a square of muslin with the halved shells. Tie into a bag.

Put the lemon juice and the pineapple in the pan with the water and the muslin bag. Bring to the boil and simmer the covered pan until the pineapple is tender. Remove the muslin bag and squeeze against the side of the pan to remove all juice.

Add the sugar and stir from time to time over a low heat until it is completely dissolved.

Bring the pan to a rolling boil and continue to boil without stirring for about 15 minutes. Test for setting or allow the sugar thermometer to reach 105°C/220°F.

Leave the jam to stand for 5 minutes before pouring into hot jars. Seal, cover and label.

Pear, Pineapple and Lemon Jam with Kirsch

MAKES ABOUT 2.8 KG/6 LB

1.4 kg/3 lb pears, peeled
1 small pineapple, peeled and cored
juice and rind of 5 lemons
1.8 kg/4 lb sugar, warmed
4–6 tbsp Kirsch

Cut the pears into slices and chop again. Chop the pineapple into pieces and put all the fruit with the lemon juice in the pan. Place the shells of the lemons in a muslin bag, tie and add to the fruit. Bring to the boil, lower the heat and simmer for about 10–15 minutes until the fruit is tender.

Add the sugar to the fruit and stir from time to time until it is completely dissolved. Bring the pan to a rolling boil and continue to boil until setting point is reached or the sugar thermometer has reached 105°C/220°F.

Pour into hot jars, seal, cover and label.

Aubergine Jam with Pecans

MAKES ABOUT 1.4 KG/3 LB

1 kg/2¼ lb aubergines
300 ml/½ pt water
1 kg/2¼ lb sugar, warmed
4 tbsp pecan nuts, chopped

Cube larger aubergines; otherwise leave small ones whole. Put into a saucepan with the water. Bring to the boil and simmer over a low heat until the vegetables are tender, about 1 hour. Most of the water will have evaporated. Add the sugar and stir from time to time over a low heat until the sugar is completely dissolved. Bring to a boil and stir in the nuts. Test for setting after about 5 minutes or when the mixture looks thick or use the sugar thermometer until it reaches 105°C/220°F.

Pour into the hot jars, seal, cover and label.

CHAPTER TWO

Conserves
and
Preserves

~

These are slightly sweeter and less set than jam. They are often made with more exotic fruits such as pineapple, banana and melon. The main difference appears to be that the texture is rather more lumpy than jam. In days gone by these were probably eaten with a spoon as a dessert as much as being spread on scones or bread.

Orange and Walnut Conserve

MAKES ABOUT 1.8 KG/4 LB

900 g/2 lb large sweet oranges, washed
1.75 ltr/3 pt water
900 g/2 lb sugar
100 g/4 oz seedless raisins
50 g/2 oz walnut pieces

Grate the rind of the oranges finely, avoiding the white pith. Cut the fruit up and put in a pan with the water, bring to the boil then lower the heat and simmer for at least 30 minutes.

Sieve the pulp through a coarse sieve and measure the amount. You will need 1.1 ltr/2 pt of orange liquid (make up the quantity with orange juice or water if necessary).

Add the sugar, stirring from time to time until completely dissolved.

Add the grated rind of the orange and the raisins, bring to the boil for about 20 minutes, stirring often.

Test for setting and then stir in the walnuts before pouring into hot jars. Seal, cover and label.

Plum, Brandy and Walnut Conserve

MAKES ABOUT 3.2 KG/7 LB

1.8 kg/4 lb plums, halved and stoned
300 ml/½ pt water
1.5 kg/3 lb sugar
100 g/4 oz walnuts, chopped
4 tbsp brandy

Place the plum stones in a small saucepan, cover with water and bring to the boil for 10 minutes.

Strain the liquid into the preserving pan, add the plums and simmer until tender, about 10–15 minutes, stirring from time to time.

Add sugar and stir over a low heat until dissolved. Bring to a rolling boil and cook for about 10 minutes, until setting point is reached or the sugar thermometer shows 105°C/220°F. Remove the pan from the heat and mix in the walnuts and the brandy.

Allow to stand for 5 minutes, pour into hot jars, seal, cover and label.

Strawberry Conserve

MAKES 2.3 KG/5 LB JAM

1.8 kg/4 lb strawberries
1.8 kg/4 lb sugar

Arrange the strawberries in a dish or bowl in layers with the sugar. Cover with clingfilm and allow to stand for 24 hours.

Next day, turn into a preserving pan and bring to the boil slowly and then boil for 5 minutes. Return to the basin, cover and allow to stand for another 48 hours.

Return to the preserving pan, bring to the boil and continue cooking this way for about 15–20 minutes, until setting point is reached.

Cool slightly, stir and then pour into hot jars. Seal, cover and label.

Rose Petal Conserve

MAKES ABOUT 450 G/1 LB

450 g/1 lb preserving sugar
1 tbsp water
450 g/1 lb rose petals, preferably deep red
2 tsp orange flower water

Put the sugar in a thick-bottomed saucepan with the water and allow the mixture to dissolve slowly over a low heat and then simmer until it becomes a syrup.

Wash the rose petals gently and dry in kitchen paper, then add them to the syrup with the orange flower water.

Simmer the mixture until it thickens slightly, but it will always be a thick syrup as opposed to a jam.

Pour into hot jars, seal, cover and label.

Keep in the refrigerator, serve with ice cream, crumpets, muffins or scones.

Saucy Rhubarb and Carrot Conserve

MAKES 1.4 KG/3 LB

450 g/1 lb tender young carrots
450 g/1 lb young rhubarb, washed
100 g/4 oz candied citrus peel
1 lemon
1 kg/2¼ lb sugar, warmed
15 g/½ oz crystallized ginger, chopped

Scrape the carrots and cut into pieces. Cut the rhubarb into pieces 2–3 cm/1 in long. Chop the citrus peel finely.

Grate the peel of the lemon, and cut away the white pith. Put the pith and pips into a muslin square and tie into a bag.

Put the carrots, rhubarb, lemon flesh and muslin bag in just enough water to cover and simmer until tender. Add the sugar and stir over a low heat until completely dissolved.

Add the citrus peel, lemon peel and chopped ginger before bringing the pan to a rolling boil. Continue until setting point is reached or the sugar thermometer reaches 105°C/220°F.

Pour into hot jars, seal, cover and label.

Rhubarb and Orange Conserve

MAKES ABOUT 2 KG/4½ LB

1.4 kg/3 lb rhubarb, washed
1.4 kg/3 lb sugar
6 tbsp lemon juice
rind and juice of 2 oranges

Cut the rhubarb into short lengths and arrange in a bowl in layers with the sugar and lemon juice. Cover with film or a saucepan lid and allow to stand for 24 hours.

Next day, tip into the preserving pan and add the rind and juice of the oranges. Stir over a low heat until the sugar is dissolved.

Raise the heat and boil rapidly until a jam-like consistency is obtained, but the conserve will not gel like jam.

Pour into hot jars, seal, cover and label.

Once opened, store in the refrigerator.

Rhubarb, Orange and Brandy Preserve

MAKES ABOUT 1.75 KG/3½ LB

900 g/2 lb rhubarb, trimmed
1 kg/2¼ lb golden granulated sugar
2 lemons
1 orange
300 ml/½ pt water
knob of butter
3 tbsp brandy or whisky

Cut the rhubarb into pieces 2–3 cm/1 in long, arrange in layers in a basin with the sugar. Leave to stand overnight. Add the squeezed juice of the lemons to the rhubarb.

Turn the debris and pips from the squeezer into a muslin square laid on a plate. Finely shred peel and pith into a small pan. Peel the orange and cut the segments away from the membrane. Add the pips to the muslin and tie into a bag. Add chopped orange segments to the rhubarb.

Shred the orange peel, add to the lemon peel in the pan and add water and muslin bag. Simmer gently, covered, for about 1 hour, until tender and liquid is well reduced (more water may be needed).

Put rhubarb mixture and peel into a preserving pan and stir over a low heat without boiling until sugar dissolves. Bring to a full rolling boil, add the butter and, at setting point, stir in brandy or whisky.

Pour into hot jars, seal, cover and label.

Honeyed Kumquat Preserve

This is a preserve which is eaten with a spoon and accompanied by lemon tea.

MAKES ABOUT 1 KG/2¼ LB

800 g/1¾ lb kumquats, washed
600 ml/1 pt water
275 g/10 oz sugar
125 ml/¼ pt (scant) clear honey

Do not peel the kumquats but make a small incision at the tip of each.

Bring the water, sugar and honey to the boil in a saucepan. Add the kumquats and cook over a low heat until tender and almost transparent (about 1 hour).

Cool and put into hot jars, seal, cover and label.

Rich Fig Preserve

MAKES ABOUT 1.4 KG/3 LB

900 g/2 lb green figs, stalks removed
1 kg/2¼ lb sugar
rind and juice of 1 lemon

Put the whole figs into a large mixing bowl. Boil the kettle and allow to stand for a few minutes. Pour the hot water over the figs and leave to soak for about 4 minutes. Drain the figs into a colander and when cool transfer to a chopping board and cut up into small pieces.

Weigh the figs and put into the preserving pan or large saucepan with the same weight of sugar. Add the rind of 1 lemon and 3 tbsp of juice. Place the pan over a low heat and allow the sugar to dissolve for about 1 hour or until a thick clear syrup appears. Add a small amount of water if the mixture becomes too thick.

Remove from the heat and, unlike other fruit jams and preserves, allow to become cold before putting into dry sterilized jars.

Seal, cover and label.

Guava and Walnut Preserve

MAKES ABOUT 550 G/1¼ LB

450 g/1 lb guavas
2 tbsp lemon juice
350 ml/12 fl oz water
450 g/1 lb golden granulated sugar
25 g/1 oz walnuts, roughly chopped

Peel the guavas thinly, discarding the ends. Cut into quarters and then cut into small pieces. Put into a pan with the lemon juice and water. Cook gently for about 30 minutes until the guavas are soft and the liquid is reduced. Rub the pan contents through a sieve to remove the seeds.

Measure the purée and make up to 600 ml/1 pt with water. Pour the purée into the cleaned pan over a low heat, then add the sugar. Stir over the low heat without boiling until the sugar is completely dissolved. Bring to the boil and stir frequently, until thick and creamy, then stir in the walnuts.

Pour into hot jars, seal, cover and label.

Nectarine and Passion Fruit Preserve

MAKES ABOUT 1 KG/2¼ LB

1.4 kg/3 lb nectarines
6 tbsp lemon juice
8–10 passion fruit
300 ml/½ pt water
1 kg/2¼ lb golden granulated sugar

Skin the nectarines, remove the stones and cut the fruit into small pieces. Put into a pan with the lemon juice.

Cut the passion fruit in half, scoop out the seeds and flesh and quarter the skins. Tie the passion fruit flesh and skins in muslin add to the pan. Pour in the water and cook gently for about 30 minutes until the nectarines are soft and the liquid is reduced. Remove the muslin and squeeze the juice into the pan. Add the sugar, stir over a low heat without boiling until completely dissolved. Bring to the boil and boil briskly until setting point is reached. Leave in the pan for 10 minutes for fruit to settle.

Pour into hot jars, seal, cover and label.

Special Pear and Apricot Preserve

MAKES 2.5 KG/5–6 LB JAM

225 g/8 oz dried apricots, halved
900 ml/1½ pt water
700 g/1½ lb sugar
juice of 2 lemons
few drops of yellow vegetable colouring
1 kg/2¼ lb pears, peeled
4 tbsp Grand Marnier liqueur

Soak the apricots in the measured water for six hours or, if using non-soak, for 1 hour. Drain, retaining the water.

Dissolve the sugar in the lemon juice and the drained apricot water. Bring to the boil and simmer until the liquid is syrupy. Add the yellow colouring to tint the syrup.

Cut the pears into thick slices and add to the pan with the halved apricots. Bring to the boil and then turn the heat down and simmer gently until the fruit is tender.

Bring to the boil again and add the Grand Marnier, boil for a few minutes, then test for setting or when the sugar thermometer has reached 105°C/220°F. Remove any scum and allow to stand for 5 minutes.

Pour into hot jars, seal, cover and label.

Spiced Green Tomato Preserve

MAKES ABOUT 5.5 KG/12 LB JAM

3 large lemons
900 ml/1½ pt water
2 cinnamon sticks
2.5 kg/5½ lb green tomatoes
2 kg/4½ lb golden granulated sugar, warmed

Wash and dry the lemons, cut into quarters lengthways and discard the pips. Slice very thinly across, retaining as much juice as possible. Put into a pan with water and cook gently for about 30 minutes until soft.

Strain, measure the liquid and make up to 400 ml/14 fl oz with more water. Return measured liquid to pan with cooked lemon and the cinnamon sticks.

Wash and dry the tomatoes, cut into fairly small pieces, removing stalk ends.

Add to pan, cook gently for about 1 hour until tomatoes are soft and the liquid has evaporated. Remove cinnamon sticks, add sugar, stir over a low heat until completely dissolved.

Pour into hot jars, seal, cover and label.

Lemony Melon Preserve

MAKES ABOUT 1.8 KG/4 LB

1 large melon or 1.4 kg/3 lb melon flesh
rind and juice of 2 lemons
1.4 kg/3 lb sugar
1 bottle commercial pectin (follow
manufacturers' directions)

Remove the flesh from the melon, discard the seeds and cut the flesh into cubes. Put the melon in a large pan with the rind and juice of the lemons, bring to the boil, turn the heat low and simmer, covered, for about 20 minutes until the melon is translucent.

Add the sugar and dissolve over a low heat, stirring from time to time. Bring to a full rolling boil for 2–3 minutes, remove from the heat and stir in the pectin.

Allow to cool, pour into hot jars, seal, cover and label.

Tropical Banana-Date Preserve

MAKES ABOUT 1.4 KG/3 LB

450 g/1 lb cooking apples, peeled,
cored and diced
3 tbsp lemon juice
400 ml/14 fl oz water
550 g/1¼ lb bananas, peeled and sliced
225 g/8 oz fresh dates, skinned,
stoned and sliced
450 g/1 lb golden granulated sugar

Put the apples in a pan and cook with lemon juice and water for about 5 minutes until soft.

Stir both the bananas and dates into the apple. Continue to cook for about 20 minutes, stirring often, until pulpy and the liquid is reduced to about 1 ltr/1¾ pt.

Stir in the sugar, dissolve over low heat, stirring all the time. Bring to the boil, stirring frequently, and boil gently until thick and the spoon leaves a space when pulled through centre. This will take 45–60 minutes.

Pour into hot jars, seal, cover and label. Eat within two months and, once open, store in the refrigerator.

Banana-Cinnamon-Rum Preserve

MAKES ABOUT 2.8 KG/6 LB

2 kg/4½ lb bananas
(about 1.4 kg/3 lb peeled)
rind and juice of 2 lemons
2 tbsp rum
2 tsp ground cinnamon
1.4 kg/3 lb sugar

Slice the peeled bananas into a bowl and add the lemon rind, juice and rum. Turn over with a fork to coat as much as possible. Layer the banana mixture with the sugar in a large bowl, cover with some clingfilm and leave to stand for 24 hours.

Next day, turn into the preserving pan, and flavour with the cinnamon and sprinkle on the remaining sugar. Stir gently over a low heat until the sugar is completely dissolved.

Bring to a rolling boil for about 5 minutes, stirring until thick and the mixture is a rich brown colour. Remove from the heat and allow to stand until the conserve thickens.

Pour into hot jars, seal, cover and label.

CHAPTER THREE

Jellies – Colourful and Bright

~

To MAKE JELLY follow the basic rules of jam making and testing. The main difference is the amount of sugar used for jelly, as this is calculated on the amount of fruit juice that is strained from the fruit. This is why the jelly recipes give an approximate amount of sugar as a guide.

Preparation for jelly making is much easier than for jam as all the washed fruit is stewed with skins, stones and cores. The fruit must be soft and mushy before straining. However, it must be remembered that the juice is strained for several hours and should be kept in a safe place away from children or animals. It is best to shut the fruit in a room overnight to avoid spillage.

EQUIPMENT FOR JELLY MAKING

Again, the equipment is exactly the same as for jam (*see* pages 8–9) with the exception of the jelly bag. This is a felt bag which can be hung over a bowl to allow the long slow dripping the fruit juice requires. These bags can be hung from an upturned stool or chair, often slung through a wooden broom handle. They are available in good kitchen shops. If no jelly bag is available then use a large sieve with two layers of muslin. Tie the fruit in the muslin like a bag and rest it in the sieve.

GENERAL GUIDELINES

For fruit high in pectin 1 kg/2¼ lb sugar is used to each litre or 1¾ pt juice. Fruits lower in pectin will use slightly less.

Do not, in any circumstances, squeeze the bag to hurry the fruit juice or the jelly will be cloudy.

Remove scum before potting or the appearance of the jelly will be impaired.

Do not tilt jelly in jars before it is cool and set.

Apple and Lemon Jelly

MAKES ABOUT 1.8 KG/4 LB

2.8 kg/6 lb apples, washed
rind and juice of 3 lemons
2.4 ltr/4 pt water
about 1.8 kg/4 lb sugar

Remove any damaged parts of the apples and cut into pieces, including the cores and skins. With a sharp knife peel the rind of the lemons thinly and then squeeze out the juice.

Put the apples, lemon rind and juice into the preserving pan with the water and bring to the boil slowly, then reduce the heat and simmer gently until the fruit is tender.

Scald the jelly bag and tip in the apple and lemon mixture. Allow to strain slowly without squeezing the bag.

Measure the apple juice into the preserving pan again and add 450 g/1 lb sugar for every 600 ml/1 pt of juice. Allow the sugar to dissolve over a low heat, stirring from time to time.

Bring the pan to a rolling boil and test for setting after 10 minutes or when the sugar thermometer reaches 105°C/220°F.

Pour into hot jars, cover, seal and label.

Jelly Marmalade

MAKES ABOUT 1.8 KG/5 LB

900 g/2 lb Seville oranges
2 lemons
2.5 ltr/4½ pt water
about 1.4 kg/3 lb sugar

Wash the fruit and dry with kitchen paper. Remove the peel thinly from the oranges and lemon with a potato peeler. Cut into thin strips to be used in the marmalade later and put in a muslin square, tied into a bag. Put into a pan with 600 ml/1 pt water and cook gently for about 1½ hours, covered if possible.

Squeeze the juice from the halved lemons.

Cut the remainder of the fruit, including what remains of the lemons, into pieces and place in a large saucepan with a lid. Add 1.3 ltr/2½ pt water and cook, covered, for about 2 hours.

Scald the jelly bag with boiling water and strain the contents of both saucepans for 30 minutes, retaining the muslin bag.

Return the contents of the jelly bag to the preserving pan, add the remaining 600 ml/1 pt of water and simmer for a further 30 minutes.

Tip the contents of the pan back into the jelly bag and allow to drip overnight.

Measure all the strained juice back into the preserving pan and add 450 g/1 lb sugar to every 600 ml/1 pt juice. Dissolve the sugar over a low heat, stirring from time to time.

Bring to a rolling boil for about 10 minutes and add some of the thinly sliced shreds of peel from the muslin bag. Test for setting or use the sugar thermometer until it reaches 105°C/220°F.

Pour into hot jars, seal, cover and label.

Seville Orange Jelly

MAKES ABOUT 2.3 KG/5 LB

1.1 kg/2½ lb Seville oranges
225 g/8 oz lemons
2 ltr/3½ pt water
about 1.4 kg/3 lb sugar

Remove the peel from the oranges and lemons with a potato peeler. Remove the pips (over a basin to catch the juice) and put into a small saucepan. Cut the remainder of the fruit into pieces. Pour 600 ml/1 pt of the water over the pips and simmer for about 30 minutes. Cover and leave until cold.

Place the lemon pieces in the preserving pan with the remaining measured water. Strain the pip water into the pan, bring to pan to the boil and simmer for 40 minutes.

Scald the jelly bag with boiling water, drain the fruit pulp overnight without squeezing the bag.

Measure the juice into a clean pan and add 450 g/1 lb sugar to every 600 ml/1 pt of juice. Put the pan on a low heat, stirring from time to time, until the sugar is completely dissolved.

Bring the pan up to a rolling boil and after 10 minutes test for setting or use the sugar thermometer until it reaches 105°C/220°F.

Allow to cool slightly then pour into hot jars, seal, cover and label.

This is best stored in small jars, to serve with poultry or duck or to make a sauce for puddings.

Lemon Jelly

This is delicious as a sauce for
sponge and suet puddings.

MAKES 2.3 KG/5 LB

1.4 kg/3 lb lemons
2 ltr/3½ pt water
about 1.4 kg/3 lb sugar

Remove the peel from the lemons with a
potato peeler. Remove the pips (over a
basin to catch the juice) and cut the
remainder of the fruit into pieces. Put
the pips in a small saucepan and pour
600 ml/1 pt of the water over them;
simmer for about 30 minutes. Cover and
leave until cold.

Place the lemon pieces in the
preserving pan with the remaining
measured water. Strain the pip water
into the pan, bring the pan to the boil
and simmer for 40 minutes.

Scald the jelly bag with boiling water,
drain the fruit pulp overnight without
squeezing the bag.

Measure the juice into a clean pan and
add 450 g/1 lb sugar to every 600 ml/1 pt
of juice. Put the pan on a low heat,
stirring from time to time, until the
sugar is completely dissolved.

Bring the pan up to a rolling boil and
after 10 minutes test for setting or use
the sugar thermometer until it reaches
105°C/220°F.

Allow to cool slightly then pour into
hot jars, seal, cover and label.

Rosemary Jelly

MAKES ABOUT 3.2 KG/7 LB

2.3 kg/5 lb cooking apples, washed
600 ml/1 pt water
4–6 tbsp fresh rosemary leaves
250 ml/8 fl oz malt vinegar
about 1.8 kg/4 lb sugar
few drops of green vegetable colouring
(optional)

Cut the apples in rough slices and put
into the preserving pan with the water.
Bring to the boil, then reduce the heat,
simmer for 5 minutes and add half the
rosemary leaves. Stir round and simmer
over a low heat for about 30 minutes
until the apples are pulpy. Add the
vinegar and simmer for a further 5
minutes.

Scald the jelly bag with boiling water
and strain the apple and rosemary pulp
through.

Measure the juice into a clean pan and
add 450 g/1 lb sugar to every 600 ml/1 pt
of juice. Put the pan on a low heat,
stirring from time to time, until the
sugar is completely dissolved.

Bring the pan up to a rolling boil and
after 5 minutes add the rest of the
rosemary, stir well and if necessary add
a few drops of green colouring. Test for
setting or use the sugar thermometer
until it reaches 105°C/220°F. Skim if
necessary.

Allow to cool slightly, then pour into
hot jars, seal, cover and label.

Cool Mint Apple Jelly

MAKES ABOUT 1.4 KG/3 LB

1.8 kg/4 lb cooking apples, washed
large bunch of fresh mint, washed
juice of 2 lemons
1 ltr/1¾ pt water
about 1.1 kg/2½ lb sugar
few drops of green vegetable colouring
(optional)

Slice the apples roughly and put in a large saucepan with half the mint, the lemon juice and the water. Bring to the boil and simmer for about 30 minutes or until the apples are soft and pulpy.

Scald the jelly bag with boiling water and strain the apple pulp through.

Measure the juice into a clean pan and add 450 g/1 lb sugar to every 600 ml/ 1 pt of juice. Put the pan on a low heat, stirring from time to time.

Remove the remaining mint leaves and chop finely (this can be done in the food processor).

Bring the pan up to a rolling boil and after 5 minutes add the mint, stir well and if necessary add a few drops of green colouring. Test for setting or use the sugar thermometer until it reaches 105°C/220°F.

Allow to cool slightly then pour into hot pots, seal, cover and label.

Gooseberry and Mint Jelly

MAKES ABOUT 2.3 KG/5 LB

1.8 kg/4 lb gooseberries, washed
large bunch of fresh mint, washed
900 g/1½ pt water
about 1.4 kg/3 lb sugar
few drops of green vegetable colouring
(optional)

Put the washed gooseberries in a large saucepan with half the mint, the lemon juice and the water. Bring to the boil and simmer for about 30 minutes or until the fruit is soft and pulpy.

Scald the jelly bag with boiling water and strain the gooseberry pulp through the bag.

Measure the juice into a clean pan and add 450 g/1 lb sugar to every 600 ml/1 pt of juice; put the pan on a low heat, stirring from time to time.

Remove the remaining mint leaves from the stalks and chop finely (this can be done in the food processor).

Bring the pan up to a rolling boil and after 5 minutes add the mint, stir well and if necessary add a few drops of green colouring. Test for setting or use the sugar thermometer until it reaches 105°C/220°F.

Allow to cool slightly, then pour into hot jars, seal, cover and label.

Gooseberry and Elderflower Jelly

MAKES ABOUT 2.3 KG/5 LB

1.8 kg/4 lb gooseberries, washed
2 tbsp lemon juice
900 g/1½ pt water
about 1.4 kg/3 lb sugar
4 large elderflower heads, well washed

Put the washed gooseberries in a large saucepan with the lemon juice and the water. Bring to the boil and simmer for about 30 minutes or until the fruit is soft and pulpy.

Scald the jelly bag with boiling water and strain the gooseberry pulp through.

Measure the juice into a clean pan and add 450 g/1 lb sugar to every 600 ml/1 pt of juice. Put the pan on a low heat stirring from time to time.

Place the elderflowers in a muslin square and tie into a bag; add to the pan while the sugar is dissolving. Bring the pan up to a rolling boil, stir well. Test for setting or use the sugar thermometer until it reaches 105°C/220°F.

Allow to cool slightly then pour into hot pots, seal, cover and label.

Medlar Jelly

The medlar is a delightful garden tree with flowing white flowers in summer and brilliant red foliage in autumn.

MAKES ABOUT 2.3 KG/5 LB

1.8 kg/4 lb medlars, washed
juice of 1 lemon
water to cover fruit
about 1.4 kg/3 lb sugar

Place the medlars in a preserving pan with the water and lemon juice; bring slowly to the boil. Reduce the heat to low and simmer the fruit until it is tender and pulpy. Allow to cool slightly.

Scald the jelly bag with boiling water, drain the fruit pulp overnight without squeezing the bag.

Measure the juice into a clean pan and add 450 g/1 lb sugar to every 600 ml/1 pt of juice. Put the pan on a low heat, stirring from time to time, until the sugar is completely dissolved.

Bring the pan up to a rolling boil and after 10 minutes test for setting or use the sugar thermometer until it reaches 105°C/220°F.

Allow to cool slightly then pour into hot jars, seal, cover and label.

Grape Jelly

MAKES 2.3 KG/5 LB

2.8 kg/6 lb green grapes
1 lemon, cut into thin slices
1.1 ltr/2 pt water
about 1.4 kg/3 lb sugar

Place the grapes and lemon slices in a large pan with the water and bring slowly to the boil. Reduce the temperature to low and simmer the fruit until it is tender and pulpy. Allow to cool slightly.

Scald the jelly bag with boiling water, drain the fruit pulp overnight without squeezing the bag.

Measure the juice into a clean pan and add 350 g/12 oz sugar to every 600 ml/1 pt of juice. Put the pan on a low heat, stirring from time to time, until the sugar is completely dissolved.

Bring the pan up to a rolling boil and after 10 minutes, test for setting or use the sugar thermometer until it reaches 105°C/220°F.

Allow to cool slightly then pour into hot jars, seal, cover and label.

Damson Jelly

MAKES ABOUT 2.3 KG/5 LB

2.8 kg/6 lb damsons, washed
1.7 ltr/3 pt water
about 1.8 kg/4 lb sugar

Put the damsons, whole, into the preserving pan with the water. Put the pan over a low heat, simmering for about 45 minutes until the damsons are tender and can be mashed.

Scald the jelly bag and drain the juice through without squeezing the bag; this is best done overnight.

Measure the juice into the preserving pan and put over a low heat. Add 450 g/1 lb of sugar to each 600 ml/1 pt juice and allow the sugar to dissolve completely over a low heat, stirring from time to time.

Bring the pan to a rolling boil for about 10 minutes. Test for setting or use the sugar thermometer to 105°C/220°F.

Pour into hot jars, seal, cover and label.

Redcurrant Jelly

MAKES ABOUT 4.5 KG/10 LB

3.5 kg/8 lb redcurrants (or a mixture
of red and white)
1.1 ltr/2 pt water
about 2.8 kg/6 lb sugar

Wash the redcurrants and put in the preserving pan with the water. Put the pan over a low heat, simmering for about 45 minutes until the currants are tender and can be mashed.

Scald the jelly bag and drain the juice through without squeezing the bag; this is best done overnight.

Measure the juice into the preserving pan and put over a low heat. Add 450 g/1 lb of sugar to each 600 ml/1 pt juice and allow the sugar to dissolve completely over a low heat, stirring from time to time.

Bring the pan to a rolling boil for about 10 minutes. Test for setting or use the sugar thermometer to 105°C/220°F.

Pour into hot jars, seal, cover and label.

Blackcurrant Jelly

MAKES ABOUT 2.3 KG/5 LB

1.8 kg/4 lb blackcurrants
600 ml/1 pt water
about 1.4 kg/3 lb sugar

Wash the blackcurrants and put in the preserving pan with the water. Put the pan over a low heat, simmering for about 45 minutes until the currants are tender and can be mashed.

Scald the jelly bag and drain the juice through without squeezing the bag; this is best done overnight.

Measure the juice into the preserving pan and put over a low heat. Add 450 g/1 lb of sugar to each 600 ml/1 pt juice and allow the sugar to dissolve completely over a low heat, stirring from time to time.

Bring the pan to a rolling boil for about 10 minutes. Test for setting or use the sugar thermometer to 105°C/220°F.

Pour into hot jars, seal, cover and label.

Gooseberry Jelly

MAKES ABOUT 1.8 KG/4 LB

1.8 kg/4 lb gooseberries, washed
1.7 ltr/3 pt water
about 1.4 kg/3 lb sugar

Place the gooseberries in a preserving pan with the water and bring to the boil. Lower the heat and simmer for about 45 minutes or until the gooseberries are tender.

Scald the jelly bag with boiling water and strain the jelly through without squeezing the bag. This is best done overnight.

Measure the juice into the preserving pan and for every 600 ml/1 pt juice, add 450 g/1 lb sugar. Heat the pan over a low heat until the sugar is completely dissolved.

Bring to a rolling boil for about 10 minutes and then test for setting or use the sugar thermometer until it reaches 105°C/220°F.

Pour into hot jars, seal, cover and label.

Quince Jelly

MAKES ABOUT 2.3 KG/5 LB

3.6 kg/8 lb quinces, washed
3.5 ltr/6 pt water
lemon juice
about 1.8 kg/4 lb sugar

Slice the quinces finely (this can be done in the food processor as they are very hard). Put into the preserving pan with 2.4 ltr/4 pt of the water. Simmer for about 1 hour until the fruit is tender.

Scald the jelly bag with boiling water and then strain the quinces through the bag for several hours. Do not squeeze the bag.

Tip the pulp back into the preserving pan, add the remaining water and bring to the boil, reduce the heat and simmer for a further 30 minutes. Strain again, mixing the two batches of juice.

Clean the preserving pan, stand over a low heat and measure the juice back into the pan. For every 600 ml/1 pt juice, add 1 tbsp lemon juice and 450 g/1 lb sugar. Stir from time to time until the sugar is completely dissolved.

Bring the pan to a rolling boil for about 10 minutes, then test for setting or use the sugar thermometer to reach 105°C/220°F.

Pour into hot jars, seal, cover and label.

Blackberry Jelly

MAKES ABOUT 4.5 KG/10 LB

3.5 kg/8 lb blackberries, washed
juice of 4 lemons
900 ml/1½ pt water
about 2.8 kg/6 lb sugar

Put the blackberries, lemon juice and water in a preserving pan and simmer until the fruit is soft and squashy.

Scald a jelly bag and strain the juice through over a 24-hour period. Do not squeeze the bag.

Measure the juice into a clean preserving pan and for each 600 ml/1 pt of strained juice weigh out 450 g/1 lb sugar. Put the pan containing the juice over a high heat until it boils, then lower the heat. Add the sugar and stir in until it is completely dissolved.

Bring the pan up to a rolling boil for about 10 minutes, then test for setting or allow the sugar thermometer to reach 105°C/220°F.

Pour into hot jars, seal, cover and label.

Apple and Blackberry Jelly

MAKES ABOUT 2.8 KG/6 LB JAM

1 kg/2¼ lb apples
2 kg/4½ lb blackberries
1.1 ltr/2 pt water
about 2.8 kg/6 lb sugar

Wash the fruit and remove any damaged parts from the apples. Cut the apples up into slices and put into the preserving pan with the blackberries and the water. Bring to the boil slowly, then lower the heat. Simmer the fruit until tender.

Scald the jelly bag with boiling water and strain the fruit through without squeezing the bag.

Measure the strained juice back into the preserving pan and add 450 g/1 lb of sugar for every 600 ml/1 pt juice. Dissolve the sugar over a low heat, stirring from time to time.

Bring to a rolling boil for about 10 minutes and then test for setting or use the sugar thermometer until it reaches 105°C/220°F.

Pour into hot jars, seal, cover and label.

Versatile Apple Jelly

This is the ideal jelly to make with windfalls, cooking apples or crab apples. Extra flavourings, such as ginger, lemon rind or cloves, can be added.

MAKES ABOUT 2.3 KG/5 LB

2.8 kg/6 lb apples (weight after removing any damaged pieces)
2 ltr/3½ pt water
juice and rind of 2 lemons
2.5 cm/1 in root ginger
about 2.3 kg/5 lb sugar

Put the washed and cleaned apples in a large pan with the water, lemon juice and rind. Bruise the ginger by bashing with something heavy and add to the fruit. Bring to the boil and lower the heat and stew until the fruit is tender.

Scald the jelly bag with boiling water and strain the fruit, without squeezing the bag or the jelly will cloud.

Measure the strained jelly back into the preserving pan and for every 600 ml/1 pt juice add 450 g/1 lb sugar.

Stir from time to time over a low heat until the sugar is dissolved. Raise the heat and when the jelly has reached a rolling boil, test for setting after 10 minutes or use the sugar thermometer until it reaches 105°C/220°F.

Pour into hot jars, seal, cover and label.

Loganberry Jelly

MAKES ABOUT 4.5 KG/10 LB

3.5 kg/8 lb loganberries, washed
900 ml/1½ pt water
about 2.8 kg/6 lb sugar

Put the loganberries in the preserving pan with the water over a low heat to simmer for about 45 minutes until the fruit is tender and can be mashed.

Scald the jelly bag and drain the juice through without squeezing the bag; this is best done overnight.

Measure the juice into the preserving pan and put over a low heat. Add 450 g/1 lb of sugar to each 600 ml/1 pt measured juice and allow the sugar to dissolve completely over a low heat, stirring from time to time.

Bring the pan to a rolling boil for about 10 minutes. Test for setting or use the sugar thermometer to 105°C/220°F.

Pour into hot jars, seal, cover and label.

Mulberry Jelly

Mulberries are low in pectin and even with the apple this jelly will set lightly.

MAKES ABOUT 1.4 KG/3 LB

450 g/1 lb mulberries, washed
450 g/1 lb cooking apples, washed
6 tbsp water
about 900 g/2 lb sugar

Place the fruit in a large pan with the water and bring slowly to the boil. Reduce the temperature to low and simmer the fruit until it is tender and pulpy. Allow to cool slightly.

Scald the jelly bag with boiling water, drain the fruit pulp overnight without squeezing the bag.

Measure the juice into a clean pan and add 450 g/1 lb sugar to every 600 ml/1 pt of juice. Put the pan on a low heat, stirring from time to time, until sugar is completely dissolved.

Bring the pan up to a rolling boil and after 10 minutes, test for setting or use the sugar thermometer until it reaches 105°C/220°F.

Allow to cool slightly then pour into hot jars, seal, cover and label.

Japonica Jelly

Japonica is a delightful shrub to grow in the garden.

MAKES ABOUT 3.2 KG/7 LB

1.4 kg/3 lb japonica fruit, washed
450 g/1 lb cooking apples or windfalls, washed
2.4 ltr/4 pt water
juice of 1 lemon
about 1.8 kg/4 lb sugar

Remove any damaged parts from the apples. Cut all the fruit up into rough slices and put into the preserving pan with the water and the lemon juice. Bring to the boil slowly then lower the heat. Simmer the fruit until tender – test by mashing with a wooden spoon.

Scald the jelly bag with boiling water and strain the fruit through without squeezing the bag.

Measure the strained juice back into the preserving pan and add 450 g/1 lb of sugar to every 600 ml/1 pt juice. Dissolve the sugar over a low heat, stirring from time to time.

Bring to a rolling boil for about 10 minutes and then test for setting or use the sugar thermometer until it reaches 105°C/220°F.

Pour into hot jars, seal, cover and label.

Spiced Grape Wine Jelly

MAKES ABOUT 2.3 KG/5 LB

1.4 kg/3 lb green grapes
1.5 kg/3 lb green apples
700 g/1½ lb cooking apples, washed and sliced
1 lemon, thinly sliced
300 ml/½ pt dry white wine
6 cardamom seeds
about 1.4 kg/3 lb sugar
4 tbsp brandy

Place all the fruit in a large pan with the water and bring slowly to the boil. Reduce the temperature to low, add the wine and cardamom pods, then allow the fruit to simmer until it is tender and pulpy. Allow to cool slightly.

Scald the jelly bag with boiling water, drain the fruit pulp overnight without squeezing the bag.

Measure the juice into a clean pan and add 450 g/1 lb sugar to every 600 ml/1 pt of juice. Put the pan on a low heat, stirring from time to time, until the sugar is completely dissolved.

Bring the pan up to a rolling boil, add the brandy and after 10 minutes test for setting or use the sugar thermometer until it reaches 105°C/220°F.

Allow to cool slightly then pour into hot jars, seal, cover and label.

Elderberry and Apple Jelly

MAKES ABOUT 1.8 KG/4 LB

1.4 kg/3 lb elderberries
1.4 kg/3 lb apples
about 1.4 kg/3 lb sugar

Strip the elderberries from the stems and put in a pan with just enough water to cover. Bring to the boil and simmer until tender.

Cut any damaged pieces from the apples and cut into slices (include skin and cores). Cook the apples in a separate pan, cover with water and simmer until tender and mushy.

Strain the juices separately or one after the other, as preferred. Mix the juice and allow 350 g/12 oz sugar for each 600 ml/1 pt of juice. Measure the juice and sugar back into the preserving pan.

Dissolve the sugar over a low heat, stirring from time to time. Bring the pan up to a rolling boil and test after 10 minutes for setting or use the sugar thermometer until it reaches 105°C/220°F.

Pour into hot jars, seal, cover and label.

Sloe Jelly

MAKES ABOUT 2.3 KG/5 LB

900 g/2 lb sloes, washed
450 g/1 lb cooking apples or
windfalls, washed
juice of 1 lemon
about 1.4 kg/3 lb sugar

Prick the sloes all over with a large needle and put into the preserving pan. Remove any damaged parts from the apples, cut into rough slices and put into the preserving pan with the sloes and the lemon juice, pour on enough water to just cover the fruit, bring to the boil then lower the heat. Simmer the fruit until tender for about 1 hour; test by mashing with a wooden spoon.

Scald the jelly bag with boiling water and strain the fruit through without squeezing the bag.

Measure the strained juice back into the preserving pan and add 450 g/1 lb of sugar to every 600 ml/1 pt juice. Dissolve the sugar over a low heat, stirring from time to time.

Bring to a rolling boil for about 10 minutes and then test for setting or use the sugar thermometer until it reaches 105°C/220°F.

Pour into hot jars, seal, cover and label.

Rowan Apple Jelly

MAKES ABOUT 800 G/1¾ LB

450 g/1 lb rowan berries
450 g/1 lb cooking apples or crab apples
1.1 ltr/2 pt water
450 g/1 lb golden granulated sugar

Strip berries free of leaves and twigs before they are weighed, then wash and dry. Scrub the apples and cut into small pieces including skin and cores. Put all the berries and apples into a pan with the water.

Cook gently, mashing occasionally, until soft and pulpy – about 1 hour. Strain through a scalded jelly bag, overnight if possible. The juice should measure about 600 ml/1 pt. Heat it in a clean pan, add sugar and stir over a low heat without boiling until completely dissolved.

Bring to the boil and boil until setting point is reached.

Pour into hot jars, seal, cover and label.

CHAPTER FOUR

Bittersweet
Marmalade

~

The WORD MARMALADE stems from the Portuguese word *marmelada*, which was a preserve made from quinces enjoyed in Europe from medieval times. In Britain the word seems to have made an appearance around the seventeenth century. A favourite tale is told of Mary Queen of Scots being served a conserve of fruits to overcome her sea-sickness on the way from France when the word was mistaken for *mal de mer*.

The preserve is now recognized as being a concoction made from citrus fruits such as grapefruit, limes, lemons and oranges.

Why bother to make it when you can buy so many varieties?

The really good quality marmalades are expensive and the homemade varieties have that extra special taste which makes the commercial products pall when tasted side by side.

WHICH FRUIT?

Bitter oranges are the most popular for marmalade in Britain as they give a sharp tang which has been enjoyed at breakfast for many years. These oranges come mainly from Seville or Málaga in Spain but some varieties now come from Italy and South Africa. Bitter oranges are recognizable by their dark orange colour and pitted skins. The season is short and have to be bought in January/February in the UK. They will keep well in the freezer (store whole, packed in freezer bags) and you can then make your marmalade when time permits. Do buy a few extra to keep in the freezer for other times of the year as they are excellent in sweet and savoury sauces.

All citrus fruits such as grapefruits, mandarins and clementines are of a good quality in the first two months of the year, so it is the best time to be making marmalade for the rest of the year. But it is always possible to have homemade marmalade at any time; just look for good quality citrus fruit and make the Three or Four Fruits Marmalade (*see* pages 48 and 49).

EQUIPMENT

***(see also* Jam Making, pages 8–9)**

You will need the following equipment: preserving pan (or very large heavy-bottomed saucepan), chopping board, sharp knife, electric or hand squeezer, wooden spoon, plate, and sterilized jars, jam-pot covers and labels.

Useful equipment, although not absolutely necessary, includes a food processor with slicing blade, a sugar thermometer and a baking tray or plastic tray.

METHODS OF MARMALADE MAKING

There are several methods for the keen marmalade maker to follow and you will hear arguments for cooking the fruit whole or cutting it up, soaking or not soaking. All of these methods work well, but give slightly different results.

Marmalade does take a bit of time to prepare and this highly satisfying task should not be undertaken when in a hurry. However, by using a microwave oven and food processor one will be able to cut the labour down to a minimum.

Marmalade roughly follows the same rules as jam making. However, citrus fruits contain a very high proportion of pectose (see page 9) in the pith and pips. These need long slow simmering in reasonable amounts of water to extract the pectin necessary for setting the marmalade.

Citrus fruits contain a fair amount of acid but, with the exception of lemons and limes, not enough a form a gel, therefore they require lemons or tartaric acid in all recipes for marmalade.

The fruit, whole or cut, can be soaked for 12–24 hours before cooking if time is available.

Prepare the fruit by washing the skins (if they seem waxy, use a clean soft brush) and wipe with a clean cloth. It is important that the skins of citrus fruits be soft *before* the sugar is added, as the sugar will render undercooked skins tough and rubbery.

The pith of sweet oranges and grapefruit tends to cloud marmalade and is better scraped out and cooked with the pips in a muslin bag.

Both methods of making marmalade, as well as cooking in the microwave oven, need long slow cooking for the skins to produce pectin before the addition of sugar.

Microwave Tip

To obtain maximum juice from citrus fruits, place the fruit in a microwave oven. Allow 10 seconds per orange or fruit. This will make the fruit easier to squeeze and increase the amount of juice. Put in about 4 or 5 at a time. Cut in half and squeeze out the juice.

Whole fruit method

1 Scrub the fruit and wipe dry with kitchen paper or a clean towel. Place in a large, heavy-bottomed saucepan or preserving pan. Cover with water (*see* recipes for amounts), bring to the boil, reduce heat to simmering and allow the fruit to cook slowly for about 2 hours until the skins are soft. This can also be done by putting the oranges in a casserole and cooking in a low oven once the water has been brought to the boil.

2 Drain the fruit in a colander, retaining the liquid – there should be about half the original amount left. Allow the fruit to cool as it is difficult to handle if it is too hot. Cut into quarters and remove the pips on to a muslin square arranged on a plate to save juice. Scrape the remaining flesh from the shells of each orange into the pan.

3 Cut the peel into thin strips with a sharp knife. Use the thinnest slicing blade on your food processor.

4 Warm the well-washed jars by placing in a low oven on several layers of newspaper. This will sterilize the jars and prevent moulds forming on the jam or marmalade during storage.

5 Place the sugar in a heatproof bowl and put into a very low oven with the jam jars for 20 minutes towards the end of simmering the fruit. This helps the sugar dissolve more easily as the fruit is not cooled down by the addition of a cold mass of sugar.

6 Add the peel and the muslin bag with the pips to the pan with the orange pulp and liquid. Bring to the boil, lower the heat and simmer for about 10 minutes. Remove the muslin bag with the pips, squeezing the juice back into the pan.

7 Add the warmed sugar. Stir from time to time over a low heat until the sugar is completely dissolved.

8 Bring the marmalade to a rolling boil and keep this brisk boil for at least 10–15 minutes or until the mixture is setting (*see* Jam Making – Setting, page 9). Alternatively, use a sugar thermometer and bring the temperature to 105°C/ 220°F. Test for setting as for jam (*see* page 11).

9 Allow to cool slightly in the pan before pouring into jars to prevent the peel rising towards the surface.

10 Put the warm jars on a tray near the pan to catch the drips, and use a funnel and jug to fill with the marmalade (*see* Jam Making, page 9). Seal, cover immediately and label.

Cut peel method

1 Scrub the fruit and wipe dry with a kitchen towel. Cut in half and squeeze out the juice.

2 Arrange a square of muslin on a plate and tip the pips and pulp from the squeezer on to the muslin. Tie into a bag.

3 Slice the peel with a very sharp knife into thin strips or put through the food processor with a thin slicing blade (*see* step 3 opposite).

4 The peel, the bag of pips and the measured water (*see* Recipes) can be put into a large pan or bowl. Allow to steep overnight if liked. This helps to soften the peel. However, if this is not practical simply put all three ingredients into a preserving pan and bring to the boil. Lower the heat and simmer for 2 hours or until the peel is softened. To test if the peel is tender, place some between two spoons and press. The peel should be fairly mushy when pressed. The liquid will be reduced by about one-third.

5 Remove the bag of pips, squeezing well to make sure the liquid content goes into the marmalade and continue as in the whole fruit method, above.

Sunny Plum Marmalade

MAKES ABOUT 2.8 KG/6 LB

*1.4 kg/3 lb plums, washed,
halved and stoned
2 large sweet oranges
1.1 kg/2½ lb sugar
300 ml/½ pt water*

Remove the stones from the plums and place the stones in a muslin square arranged on a plate.

Cut the oranges in half and squeeze the juice (20 seconds in the microwave for maximum juice extraction). Tip the pips and pulp in the squeezer into the muslin. Remove as much of the pith as possible from the oranges and place in the muslin. Tie into a bag. Cut the peel into thin strips.

Place the plums, orange peel, juice and pips into the preserving pan and pour on the water. Bring to the boil and simmer for at least 1 hour to tenderize the peel.

Add the sugar and dissolve over a low heat stirring from time to time.

Bring to the boil when the sugar is dissolved and boil until setting point is reached for 105°C/220°F on the sugar thermometer.

Allow to cool slightly and pour into hot jars. Seal, cover and label.

Dundee Marmalade

MAKES ABOUT 2.8 KG/6 LB

1 kg/2¼ lb Seville oranges
juice of 2 lemons
2.4 ltr/4 pt water
2 kg/4½ lb sugar

Cut the oranges in quarters and remove the pips into a bowl. Scoop out the remaining inside into another bowl. Cut the skin into very thin strips with a sharp knife. This stage can be done in a food processor with a thin slicing blade by packing the skins sideways in the tube.

Place the pips in a nylon sieve and strain all the juice into the measured water. Place the pips in a muslin bag. Strain the pulp in the same sieve to remove most of the juice and place the pulp in the bag with the pips. Tie the bag. Add the cut peel to the water, orange juice and lemon juice, mix well, then add the muslin bag and boil until the peel is very tender. This will take at least one hour and the liquid should be reduced by about one third to one half. Remove the muslin bag.

Now add the warmed sugar and stir over a low heat until the sugar is dissolved. Bring to a rolling boil and then test after 10 minutes for a set. Alternatively, use the sugar thermometer to check when the temperature reaches 105°C/220°F.

Allow to stand for a few minutes then pour into hot jars, seal, cover and label.

Lime Marmalade

MAKES ABOUT 4.5 KG/10 LB

1.4 kg/3 lb limes
2 ltr/3½ pt water
2.8 kg/6 lb sugar, warmed

Cut the fruit in half (remember to put in the microwave oven if you have one, *see* page 46) and squeeze out all the juice and pips. Tip the pips from the squeezer into a muslin square. Scrape the pulp out of the shells and squeezer and chop into a large bowl. Cut the peel into thin strips and add to the pulp. Cover the contents of the bowl with the measured cold water and soak overnight.

Put the peel and water into the preserving pan with the juice and pips wrapped in muslin. Bring to the boil and simmer briskly for about 2 hours until the peel is soft.

Remove the muslin with the pips and add the sugar. Stir over a low heat until the sugar is dissolved then bring up to the boil and allow to boil briskly until the marmalade begins to set when tested or has reached 105°C/220°F on the sugar thermometer.

Allow to cool slightly, pour into hot jars, seal, cover and label.

VARIATION

Lemon Marmalade

Make exactly as Lime Marmalade, substituting the same quantity of lemons for limes. Lemon and Lime Marmalade can be made using half limes and half lemons.

Three Fruits Marmalade

MAKES 4.5 KG/10 LB

2 grapefruit (about 700 g/1½ lb)
2 sweet oranges (about 350 g/12 oz)
4 lemons
3.5 ltr/6 pt water, warmed
2.8 kg/6 lb sugar, warmed

Cut the fruit in half and squeeze the juice. Lay a square of muslin on a plate and tip in the pips and pulp from the squeezer. If a clear marmalade is wanted cut or scrape some of the pith from the grapefruit and oranges and place it in with the pips. Tie up the four corners of the muslin to make a bag.

Cut the peel into thin strips with a sharp knife or use a thin slicing blade in a food processor.

Measure the water into the pan and then add the peel with the juice and the muslin bag to the pan and bring to the boil. Simmer until the peel is very soft; this will take about 2 hours. The liquid will be reduced by about one third. Remove the bag with the pips, allow to cool and discard the contents.

Add the warmed sugar and stir from time to time, over a low heat, until it is completely dissolved.

Bring the marmalade to a rolling boil and continue boiling briskly until setting point is reached. This should be in about 10–15 minutes or when the sugar thermometer reaches 105°C/220°F. Test for setting. When ready, allow to cool slightly for about 10 minutes to prevent the peel rising to the top.

Pour into hot jars, seal, cover and label.

Bittersweet Marmalade

This is an excellent marmalade and can be made all the year round.

MAKES ABOUT 3.5 KG/8LB

4 lemons
2 sweet oranges
2 grapefruit
3.5 ltr/6 pt water
2.8 kg/6 lb light muscovado sugar, warmed

Wash the fruit and dry with a clean towel or kitchen paper. If possible, put into the microwave oven for 10 seconds per fruit. Halve the fruit and squeeze out all the juice.

Lay out a square of muslin on a plate and tip all the seeds on to the muslin. Scrape out as much of the white pith as you can from the grapefruit and oranges and put into the muslin. Tie into a bag.

Cut the peel into thin strips with a sharp knife or in the food processor using a thin slicing blade, and put into the preserving pan with the juice, the water and the muslin bag.

Bring to the boil, lower the heat and simmer for about 2 hours. Stir from time to time. Squeeze the muslin bag to remove as much liquid as possible before discarding. Tip in the sugar and stir over a low heat from time to time until dissolved.

Boil rapidly for about 15 minutes until setting point is reached or the sugar thermometer reads 105°C/220°F. Test for setting, allow to cool slightly.

Pour into hot jars, seal, cover and label.

Four Fruits Marmalade

MAKES ABOUT 4.5 KG/10 LB

2 grapefruit
4 lemons
2 Seville oranges
2 tangerines
3.5 ltr/6 pt water
2.8 kg/6 lb preserving sugar

Remove the peel from all the fruit with a sharp knife, taking very little pith with the skin. This method is used to make a less cloudy marmalade as the grapefruit and tangerine pith tends to cloud the marmalade. Cut the peel into thin shreds.

Lay a large square of muslin on a plate. Cut the fruit in halves and squeeze out the juice. Put the pith and left-over pulp into the muslin. Tie the bag. Place the peel, juice, bag and water in a bowl and allow to stand for 12 hours.

Tip the contents of the bowl into the preserving pan and bring to the boil then allow to simmer for about 2 hours.

Squeeze out the bag and discard the contents. Add the warmed sugar and stir from time to time until dissolved.

Bring to a rolling boil and continue to boil for 10–15 minutes until setting point is reached or 105°C/220°F on the sugar thermometer.

Allow to stand for 10 minutes then pour into the hot jars. Seal, cover and label.

Tomato Marmalade

MAKES 3 KG/6–7 LB

2 kg/4½ lb ripe tomatoes
3 lemons
1.8 kg/4 lb preserving sugar
300 ml/½ pt water

Place the tomatoes in a large bowl and pour boiling water over. Remove the tomatoes with a fork and pull the skins off. Slice thickly.

Slice the lemons, remove and discard the pips. Put the sugar in a pan with the water and bring up to the boil stirring from time to time. When dissolved, boil briskly for 6 minutes. Lower the heat and add the tomatoes and lemons, bring back to the boil for 30–40 minutes until thick. Remove any scum from the surface and the lemon rind can also be removed at the end of the cooking time with a slotted spoon.

Allow to cool slightly and pour into hot jars, seal, cover and label.

Grapefruit Marmalade

MAKES ABOUT 2 KG/4½ LB

2 grapefruit (about 700 g/1½ lb)
2 large lemons
1.75 ltr/3 pt water
1.4 kg/3 lb sugar, warmed

Squeeze the juice from the fruit (for maximum extraction, place in a microwave oven (*see* page 46). Scoop out the pulp and chop up finely. Scrape some of the pith from the lemon skins (grapefruit pith tends to make marmalade go cloudy) and put with the lemon and grapefruit pips in a muslin square, tied up like a bag. Place the fruit peel, juice, muslin bag and water into the preserving pan and bring to the boil. Reduce the heat and simmer until the peel is tender.

Remove the muslin bag with the pips and pith and add the sugar. Reduce the heat and dissolve the sugar over a low heat, stirring from time to time.

When the sugar is completely dissolved turn up the heat until the marmalade is boiling briskly. Continue to boil for 10–15 minutes until the mixture starts to set. Alternatively boil until the sugar thermometer reaches 105°C/220°F.

Allow to cool slightly and then pour into hot jars. Seal, cover and label.

Tutti-Frutti Marmalade

This mixture has a really delicate flavour and is ideal for those who enjoy an alternative to the bitter orange flavour.

MAKES ABOUT 2.3 KG/5 LB

1 grapefruit
1 sweet orange
1 lemon
1.5 ltr/2½ pt water
1 large cooking apple
2 pears
1.4 kg/3 lb sugar, warmed

If you have a microwave oven, place the grapefruit, orange and lemon in on full power for 40 seconds. Squeeze the fruit to remove the juice and tip the pips and pulp on to a square of muslin and spread over a plate. Scrape as much of the pith from the grapefruit and sweet orange as you can manage. Place it in the muslin with the pips and tie into a bag.

Cut the peel into thin strips and put into a large saucepan or preserving pan with the water and the muslin bag. Bring to the boil and then simmer until the peel is soft (about 2 hours).

Remove the muslin bag, squeezing well and add the peeled and diced apple and pear to the pan. Mix well and bring the mixture to the boil, lower the heat and add the warmed sugar. Stir from time to time until the sugar is dissolved completely.

Bring the pan to a rolling boil and allow to cook briskly for 10–15 minutes before testing for setting.

Allow the marmalade to stand for 5–10 minutes, then pour into hot jars. Seal, cover and label.

Microwave Marmalade

This is an excellent way to make a small amount of marmalade. It can be made while doing other things as there is no fear of it boiling over. This method is only slightly quicker than the conventional methods. However, the microwave oven does time the cooking for you.

MAKES 2.75 KG/6 LB

900 g/2 lb Seville oranges
1 lemon
1.75 ltr/3 pt water
1.6 kg/3½ lb sugar

Place the oranges and lemon in the microwave and turn on high for 3 minutes. Cut the fruit in half and squeeze the juice. Tip the pips from the squeezer on to a muslin square placed over a plate. Scrape out any pulp left in the fruit skins with some of the pith and put in the muslin with the pips. Tie the muslin into a bag.

Cut the peel into thin strips and place in a 3.5-ltr/6-pt bowl. Add the juice and the muslin bag with the measured water. Heat in the oven on full power for about 1 hour. Stir from time to time. Test the peel to make sure that it is soft.

Stir in the sugar and put back into the oven for 10 minutes and then stir again. Make sure that the sugar is completely dissolved before the final boiling.

Put the bowl back into the oven for 30 minutes on full power and then stir again. Return to the oven for a further 15 minutes and test for setting. If required, cook for a further 10 minutes.

Remove any scum from the surface and allow to stand for 5 minutes then pour into warmed jars. Seal, cover and label.

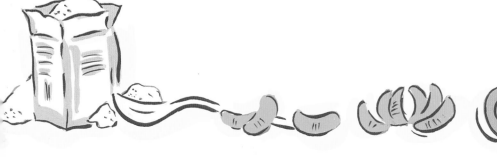

Devil's Marmalade

This is another treat for real marmalade lovers.

MAKES ABOUT 4.5 KG/10 LB

1.4 kg/3 lb Seville oranges
2 lemons
3.5 ltr/6 pt water
2.8 kg/6 lb soft dark brown sugar, warmed
2 tbsp treacle

The fruit can be treated by either method of softening but the whole fruit method is always successful (*see* pages 46–47). Wash the fruit and put in the preserving pan with the measured water, bring to the boil and simmer until the skins are soft (about 2 hours). Drain the fruit and allow to cool, retain the cooking liquid.

Cut the fruit in quarters and remove the pips into a bowl. Scrape out the pulp into another bowl (it is best to do this as you can then catch any stray pips). Measure 1.75 ltr/3 pt of orange water into the pan, add the pulp.

Scrape some of the pith into the pip bowl and then cut the peel into thin strips and add to pulp in the pan. Add the pips and pith wrapped in a muslin bag and bring to the boil.

Lower the heat, add the warmed sugar and stir from time to time over a low heat until the sugar is completely dissolved. Add the treacle.

Turn up the heat and bring the fruit and liquid to a rolling boil. Keep this brisk boil for 10–15 minutes until setting point is reached. Alternatively, use the sugar thermometer until it reaches 105°C/220°F.

Allow the marmalade to settle off the heat for about 10 minutes and then fill the hot jars. Seal, cover and label.

Cottage Marmalade

This is a slightly bitter marmalade with a whisky flavour for the marmalade connoisseur.

MAKES ABOUT 2.3 KG/5 LB

1 kg/2¼ lb Seville oranges
1 lemon
1.7 kg/3¾ lb preserving sugar
150 ml/5 fl oz whisky

Place the oranges and lemon in a large saucepan or preserving pan, add 2 ltr/3½ pt of water. Bring to the boil and simmer until the oranges are tender (about 1–2 hours).

Retain the orange water and lift the oranges into a colander, allow to drain and cool.

Cut the oranges in half and remove the pips into a bowl. The flesh should be scraped out with a spoon into another bowl and the peel placed on a chopping board. Cut the peel into thin strips. Tip the pips into a nylon sieve and press any loose flesh into the juice bowl.

Weigh 450 g/1 lb of flesh and peel, tip into a pan with 600 ml/1 pt orange water. Add 700 g/1½ lb sugar. Continue to measure out batches of solid and liquid, adding 700 g/1½ lb for each batch. Dissolve the sugar over a low heat, stirring from time to time.

Bring to a rolling boil and boil for about 35 minutes until setting or the mixture reaches 105°C/220°F on a sugar thermometer. Add whisky about 10 minutes before the end of the cooking time. Test, finally, on a chilled saucer.

Allow to stand for a few minutes then pour into hot jars, seal, cover and label.

CHAPTER FIVE

Fruit Cheeses, Butters and Curds

~

THESE ARE OLD-FASHIONED preserves made with a mixture of fruit purée and sugar. They have been around Britain for several hundred years but are often associated with the early settlers in America. They are popular all over the USA and are a particular speciality of the Pennsylvanian Dutch community.

They can be served as a sweetmeat or with cheese, and they are popular in country districts as they can be made when there is a glut of fruit. The proportion of sugar is high but not as high as in jam making.

FRUIT CHEESES

Fruit cheeses are usually made in moulds or containers; this allows the cheese to be turned out whole and it can be served decorated with fresh fruit. Store as for jam, taking the same care with storage, and the flavour will improve with keeping. Serve fruit cheeses with fresh crusty bread and butter and a favourite dairy cheese.

FRUIT BUTTERS

This is yet another way of using up excess fruit, especially apples, and the mixtures are often spiced with allspice, cloves, cinnamon or mace.

This mixture is softer than fruit cheese and should be kept in jars as it does not unmould like the fruit cheese. Storage periods are shorter unless well sealed with waxed covers or Kilner jars. Keep in the refrigerator once opened and eat within one week.

CURDS AND MINCEMEAT

These are not strictly fruit preserves as they contain other ingredients. Fruit curds do not keep as well as jam. They should be carefully stored as they contain eggs and butter.

Once the curd is open, it should be eaten quickly or stored in the refrigerator. Curds will keep for about a month in a cool place or for three months in the refrigerator, unopened.

Damson Cheese

MAKES ABOUT 1.5 KG/3 LB

1.4 kg/3 lb damsons
150 ml/¼ pt water
1 tsp allspice
sugar

Place the damsons and the water in a large saucepan with a lid and simmer the fruit for about 40 minutes or until tender. Rub the fruit through a sieve to make a purée and measure it back into the pan or use a preserving pan.

For every 600 ml/1 pt of purée add 450 g/1 lb sugar. Return to a low heat and add the allspice, mix well. Simmer, stirring all the time until the mixture is really thick. Draw a spoon across the pan and it should leave a line.

The moulds or jars should be sterilized and warm. They can be brushed with glycerine to help the fruit cheese to unmould. Seal, cover and label.

VARIATION

Blackcurrant Cheese
Quince Cheese
Gooseberry Cheese
Medlar Cheese

These are all popular country favourites which can be made using the same recipe as Damson Cheese. Other fruits can also be used.

Creamy Lemon Curd

This makes the ideal quantity for the inside of a sandwich cake with a little left over for tea time.

MAKES 225 G/8 OZ

1 egg
1 lemon
100 g/4 oz granulated sugar
50 g/2 oz butter

Beat egg with lemon juice and strain into a small saucepan. Add sugar and butter to the pan and stand over a low heat until butter is melted and sugar dissolved. Raise heat to low/medium and stir constantly until mixture just starts to bubble.

Remove from the heat immediately and pour into hot jars, seal, cover and label.

Classic Lemon Curd

As curd does not keep as well as jam, it is often best to store it in small pots. It can also be frozen in polythene boxes for up to six months.

MAKES ABOUT 900 G/2 LB

grated rind and strained juice of 4 lemons
4 eggs, well beaten
100 g/4 oz softened unsalted butter
450 g/1 lb golden granulated sugar

Put all the ingredients into a basin standing in a pan of simmering water or a double boiler. Stir steadily until the sugar melts, then cook over a very low heat, stirring frequently, until the curd thickens; do not allow to clot.

Pour the curd into hot jars, seal, cover and label.

Cider Apple Butter

MAKES ABOUT 2.8 KG/6 LB

2.8 kg/6 lb crab apples, washed
1.1 ltr/2 pt water
1.1 ltr/2 pt cider
sugar
1 tsp ground cloves
1 tsp ground cinnamon
½ tsp allspice
grated rind of 1 lemon

Cut any damaged parts of the fruit away and cut roughly into slices. Put the apples into the preserving pan with the water and cider. Bring the pan to the boil and simmer until the fruit is soft and pulpy. Allow to cool slightly and then rub through a nylon sieve.

Weigh the apple pulp back into the preserving pan and allow 350 g/12 oz sugar for each 600 ml/1 pt. Simmer for 10 minutes then add the spices and grated rind and continue cooking until thick and no liquid remains.

Pour into warm jars, seal, cover and label.

Gooseberry Curd

MAKES 1.4 KG/3 LB

1.4 kg/3 lb gooseberries, washed
75 ml/3 fl oz water
75 g/3 oz butter
4 eggs, beaten
550 g/1¼ lb sugar

Put the gooseberries into a large saucepan with the water and simmer until the fruit is soft and pulpy (about 25–30 minutes). Rub the gooseberries through a coarse sieve, discard the skins.

Using a double boiler or a large heatproof bowl over a saucepan of hot water, put in the butter and allow to melt, then stir in the beaten eggs, sugar and gooseberry purée. Whisk or stir the mixture constantly until it becomes thick.

Pour into hot jars, seal, cover and label.

Orange Curd

MAKES ABOUT 1.4 KG/3 LB

5 medium to large oranges
1 tbsp lemon juice
2 tsp orange flower water
350 g/12 oz butter, cut into small pieces
900 g/2 lb caster sugar
8 eggs, beaten

Peel the rind of the oranges and then squeeze the juice. (If possible, microwave for 40 seconds before squeezing for maximum extraction.)

Put the juice, rind, lemon juice, orange flower water, butter and sugar into a double boiler or large bowl over a large saucepan half filled with boiling water on a medium heat.

Use a whisk or electric beater and beat in the eggs a little at a time until the curd has thickened; this may take about 30 minutes.

Strain through a coarse sieve to remove the orange rind. Return to the pan, scraping as much as possible back with a plastic scraper.

Reheat for 5 minutes and pour into hot jars, seal, cover and label.

Cranberry Cheese

Make this fruit cheese with the extra cranberries which are usually around at Christmas or Easter. Serve with turkey or goose.

MAKES ABOUT 1.4 KG/3 LB

1.4 kg/3 lb cranberries
1 ltr/1¾ pt water
1.4 kg/3 lb sugar
rind and juice of 1 orange
2 tsp lemon juice
1 tsp ground cinnamon
¼ tsp ground mace

Rinse the cranberries if necessary and put into a pan covered with the water. Simmer, covered, for about 30 minutes until the fruit is very soft. Mash the fruit with a wooden spoon or a potato masher from time to time to hasten the cooking and release the juice.

Put the mixture through a food processor or liquidizer. Sieve the purée into a clean pan. If there is too much liquid, boil for a few minutes to reduce.

Add the sugar, simmer over a low heat stirring constantly until the sugar has dissolved. Stir in the orange rind, fruit juices and spices, bring to the boil and cook until thick.

Put into warm moulds or jars, seal, cover and label.

Blueberry Curd

MAKES 1 KG/2¼ LB

450 g/1 lb blueberries, washed
175 g/6 oz butter
450 g/1 lb granulated sugar
4 medium to large eggs
few drops of red vegetable colouring

Put the blueberries into a covered pan with 2 tbsp water and simmer until the fruit is tender. Push through a sieve and then pour the fruit juice into a double boiler or thick-bottomed saucepan with the butter and sugar. Stir with a wooden spoon or whisk until the sugar is dissolved.

Beat the eggs together in a bowl and strain through a fine sieve into the blueberry mixture. Continue to stir or whisk until the contents are thick and coat the back of a wooden spoon.

Pour into hot jars, seal, cover and label. Keeping qualities as for Lemon Curd.

VARIATION

Blackberry Curd/ Blackcurrant Curd

Blackberries (brambles) or blackcurrants can also be used to make a flavoured curd using the same quantities as blueberries.

Plum Gumbo

MAKES 2.8 KG/6 LB

1.4 kg/3 lb plums, washed
300–600 ml/½–1 pt water
2 oranges, washed
450 g/1 lb seedless raisins
1.4 kg/3 lb sugar

Cut the plums in half and put into a large saucepan with the water. Slice the oranges very thinly and add to the plums, cover and simmer until the fruit is really soft and mushy.

Rub through a sieve and return to the rinsed pan with the sugar and raisins. Simmer until the mixture is really thick, stirring all the time.

Turn into warmed moulds or jars, seal, cover and label.

Grapefruit Curd

MAKES 1 KG/2¼ LB

2 pink grapefruit, washed, and rind finely grated
175 g/6 oz butter
450 g/1 lb granulated sugar
4 medium to large eggs
few drops of red vegetable colouring (optional)

Squeeze the grapefruit and place rind and juice into a double boiler or thick-bottomed saucepan with the butter and sugar. Stir with a wooden spoon or whisk until the sugar is dissolved.

Beat the eggs together in a bowl and strain through a fine sieve into the grapefruit mixture. Continue to stir or whisk until the contents are thick and coat the back of a wooden spoon. Add a few drops of colouring, if liked, and stir well.

Pour into hot jars, seal, cover and label. The keeping qualities are the same as for Lemon Curd.

Lemon Marrow Curd

MAKES ABOUT 1.4 KG/3 LB

1 medium-sized marrow, peeled
900 g/2 lb sugar
finely grated rind of 2 lemons
100 g/4 oz butter

Cut the marrow in quarters and remove the seeds. Weigh about 1 kg/2 lb of the marrow and boil in a saucepan with 1 ltr/1¾ pt water and 1 tsp salt.

Strain the marrow through a sieve and allow to drain thoroughly. Mash the marrow into a large saucepan and when it is puréed add the sugar, the grated lemon rind and the butter. Stir over a gentle heat until the butter is dissolved,

then boil the marrow mixture until you have a smooth paste.

Put into small hot jars, seal, cover and label. This curd can also be frozen in small plastic pots.

Ruby Curd

MAKES 1 KG/2¼ LB

4 blood oranges, washed and rind finely grated
175 g/6 oz butter
450 g/1 lb granulated sugar
4 medium to large eggs
few drops of red vegetable colouring (optional)

Squeeze the orange and place rind and juice into a double boiler or thick-bottomed saucepan with the butter and sugar. Stir with a wooden spoon or whisk until the sugar is dissolved.

Beat the eggs together in a bowl and strain through a fine sieve into the orange mixture. Continue to stir or whisk until the contents are thick and coat the back of a wooden spoon. Add a few drops of colouring, if liked, and stir well.

Pour into hot jars, seal, cover and label. Keeping qualities as for Classic Lemon Curd.

CHAPTER SIX

Chutneys

~

THIS CONDIMENT IS now popular all over the world but originated in India with the word "chutney" coming from the Hindi word *chatni*. These savoury mixtures of fruits and vegetables are preserved in vinegar, spice and salt.

Chutneys are easy to make at any time of the year as they can be made with dried fruits as well as fresh. There is enormous scope for imagination and individual tastes in this type of preserving as different ingredients can be used to create different flavours. Chutneys can be mild or fiery hot depending on taste.

Dishes of chutney add piquancy to cold collations of meat or fish with salad as well as improving cheese and bread lunches and sandwiches. Curries and oriental dishes are often served accompanied by spicy chutneys.

Fruits such as apples, gooseberries, plums, peaches, apricots, green and red tomatoes are good basic ingredients for chutney, mixed with onions, garlic, dates, raisins, chillies, spices and sugar. The whole mixture of chosen ingredients is then preserved in vinegar. Unlike other methods of preservation the fruit does not need to be in perfect condition providing all damaged pieces are removed.

The onion is the toughest of the ingredients and it is advisable to cook the prepared onion in a little water before adding the remaining ingredients. Brown sugar is often used for a dark rich colour when cooking chutney. Use ground spices, otherwise whole spices should be wrapped in muslin before adding.

A good chutney should have a reasonably smooth texture with a mellow flavour. The basic ingredients can be cut up or minced fairly small (apples, plums etc. can be chopped in the food processor for a few seconds) and ingredients such as raisins, dates and sultanas will give character to the texture.

Long slow cooking is essential for a good mellow flavour and the chutney should be allowed to mature in the jar for at least three months.

EQUIPMENT

You will need a large pan for chutney, a preserving pan is ideal. Do not use brass, copper or iron pans as they will react with the vinegar. Similarly use only hair, nylon or stainless steel sieves.

Keep one long-handled wooden spoon for chutney as the wood will absorb some flavour and it should not be used for other cooking.

Any heatproof jars are suitable for bottling chutney. Wash thoroughly and dry in the oven as for jam jars (*see* page 11). Pour the chutney into the jars with a jug or ladle while it is hot.

Paper jam covers are not suitable as the vinegar will evaporate and the top of the chutney will be dried and spoiled. Use waxed paper or two layers of greaseproof to cover the chutney when it is hot. If clip-on lids are not available tie a piece of greaseproof or waxproof paper round the top. Metal lids can be used to fit commercial jars but should be lined with clingfilm and therefore only used to cover cold chutney.

The most simple method is to first cover the hot chutney completely with sheets of waxed paper. Allow to cool and then seal with clingfilm. To make discs for the tops, fold a sheet of paper several times into a square and draw a circle from the top of a jar. Cut round.

Tomato Chutney with Cinnamon and Cayenne

MAKES ABOUT 3.5 KG/8 LB

2.8 kg/6 lb ripe tomatoes, skinned
225 g/8 oz onions, thinly sliced
4 level tsp whole allspice
1 stick cinnamon
1 level tsp cayenne pepper
1 tbsp salt
300 ml/½ pt malt vinegar
350 g/12 oz light muscovado sugar

Cut the tomatoes in quarters and place in a large pan, together with the onions. Put the allspice and cinnamon in a square of muslin and tie into a bag. Add the muslin bag, cayenne pepper and salt to the tomato mixture. Cook gently, stirring occasionally, until the mixture is pulpy.

Add vinegar and sugar and simmer until the mixture thickens (this may take up to an hour, but do bear in mind that tomato chutney should not be as thick as other varieties of chutney). Remove the muslin bag.

Pour into hot dry jars. Seal with waxed discs, cover and label.

Green Tomato Chutney

MAKES ABOUT 2.5 KG/5–6 LB

1.4 kg/3 lb tomatoes, green or under-ripe
6 large onions, very thinly sliced
3 large cooking apples
600 ml/1 pt malt vinegar
225 g/8 oz raisins
450 g/1 lb muscovado sugar
1 tsp ground ginger
1½ tsp salt
1 tsp freshly ground black pepper
25 g/1 oz pickling spice

Slice the tomatoes. Put the tomatoes and onions into a large bowl and sprinkle with salt. Leave overnight.

Next day, drain away juice which will have collected. Peel, core and chop the apples. Put with the other ingredients into a large saucepan or preserving pan.

Stir over a moderate heat until the sugar dissolves, then simmer contents of pan gently for about 2 hours or until the chutney is thick, rich and dark brown in colour.

Pour into hot jars, cover each with a disc of waxed paper and cover jars with vinegar-proof tops. Label with the date and allow to mature for at least three months.

Cucumber Relish with Cumin

MAKES ABOUT 1.8 KG/4 LB

900 g/2 lb cucumber, unpeeled
2 Spanish onions
1 red pepper, deseeded
3 tbsp salt
450 ml/¾ pt cider vinegar
350 g/12 oz light muscovado sugar
½ tsp ground turmeric
2 tsp black mustard seeds
1½ tsp ground cumin

Thinly slice the cucumber, onions and pepper (this can be done in a food processor). Layer the vegetables in a bowl and add the salt. Cover and leave for 3 hours. Tip into a colander and rinse well.

Put in a large pan, add the cider vinegar and bring to the boil. Simmer, uncovered, for 20 minutes until the vegetables are tender. Stir in the sugar until dissolved. Add the turmeric, mustard seeds and cumin and then stir. Bring to the boil.

Remove from the heat and allow to cool. Ladle into hot jars, seal with waxed discs and cover with clingfilm when cold. Label.

Peppery Pumpkin Chutney

MAKES ABOUT 1.8 KG/4 LB

1.8 kg/4 lb piece of pumpkin
450 g/1 lb tomatoes, skinned and chopped
225 g/8 oz onions, chopped
2 cloves garlic, crushed
700 g/1½ lb demerara sugar
2 tbsp salt
1 tsp ground ginger
1 tsp pepper
1 tsp allspice
600 ml/1 pt vinegar (white wine, cider or rice vinegar) or distilled water

Cut the skin off the pumpkin and remove the seeds and threads. Slice the flesh into flat pieces about 1 cm/½ in square and 5 mm/¼ in thick. Put them into a large pan, preferably enamel or stainless steel, or a preserving pan. Add the tomatoes, onions and garlic to the pan with the sugar, salt, spices and vinegar or water. Allow the sugar to dissolve over a low heat, stirring all the time.

Bring the mixture to the boil, then let it simmer, uncovered, for about 1½ hours, or until it is thick and glossy-looking,

like bought mango chutney. It will still be runny but will not look watery. Stir the mixture frequently towards the end of the cooking time to prevent sticking.

Pour into hot jars and cover immediately with airtight and vinegar-proof tops. Label.

Hot Indian Chutney

MAKES ABOUT 2 KG/4½ LB

700 g/1½ lb (prepared weight) cooking apples, peeled, cored and sliced
450 g/1 lb onions, skinned and finely chopped
700 g/1½ lb dark muscovado sugar
1.5 ltr/2½ pt malt vinegar
450 g/1 lb seedless raisins, chopped
4 cloves garlic, skinned and crushed
4 level tsp salt
2 level tbsp ground ginger
3 level tbsp mustard powder
2 level tbsp paprika
1 level tbsp ground coriander

Place all the ingredients in a preserving pan. Bring to the boil, then reduce the heat and simmer gently for about 3 hours, uncovered, stirring occasionally, until no excess liquid remains and the chutney is thick and pulpy.

Spoon into prepared jars and cover immediately with airtight and vinegar-proof tops. Label.

Marrow and Apple Chutney

MAKES ABOUT 2.8 KG/6 LB

1.8 kg/4 lb marrow, peeled and chopped
75 g/3 oz salt
900 g/2 lb cooking apples, peeled, cored and finely chopped
450 g/1 lb shallots or onions, skinned and chopped
450 g/1 lb light muscovado sugar
1.1 ltr/2 pt distilled vinegar
1 level tsp ground ginger
15 g/½ oz pickling spice

Layer the marrow pieces into a large bowl with the salt and leave covered for 12 hours or overnight.

Rinse the marrow pieces, drain off the water and put the marrow into a preserving pan. Add the apples, shallots, sugar, vinegar, ginger and spice. Bring to the boil, then reduce the heat and simmer gently, uncovered, for about 2 hours, stirring from time to time, until the chutney becomes thick with no excess liquid.

Pour into prepared hot jars while warm and cover immediately with airtight and vinegar-proof tops. Label.

Tamarind Chutney

MAKES 225 G/8 OZ

50 g/2 oz dried tamarind
300 ml/½ pt boiling water
2 tsp fresh ginger root, scraped and grated
1 tbsp fresh lemon juice
1 tsp dark muscovado sugar
1 tsp salt
1–2 tbsp finely chopped fresh coriander

Place the tamarind in a small bowl and pour the boiling water over it. Leave to soak for about an hour, stirring and mashing occasionally. Rub through a fine sieve, pressing down hard to extract all the pulp.

Add the ginger, lemon juice, sugar and salt. Stir together well. Cover and store in the fridge, it will keep for at least a week.

Sprinkle with chopped coriander just prior to serving.

Spiced Peach and Orange Chutney

MAKES ABOUT 1.6 KG/3½ LB

1 kg/2¼ lb peaches, peeled, quartered and stoned
2 onions, peeled and thinly sliced
3 large cloves garlic, crushed
grated rind and juice of 2 oranges
225 g/8 oz sultanas
175 g/6 oz chopped preserve ginger
100 g/4 oz flaked almonds
1 tsp ground allspice
1 tsp ground cinnamon
2 tsp salt
600 ml/1 pt white wine vinegar
225 g/8 oz molasses sugar

Place the peaches in a large saucepan. Add all the ingredients and stir over a low heat until the sugar is dissolved. Bring to the boil, stirring all the time, lower the heat and simmer gently for about 1½ hours or until the chutney is thick, stirring from time to time to avoid sticking.

Ladle into hot jars, seal with airtight, vinegar-proof covers and label.

Red Tomato and Raisin Chutney

MAKES ABOUT 1.8 KG/4 LB

2.8 kg/6 lb red tomatoes, skinned and sliced
450 g/1 lb onion, skinned and minced
1 clove garlic, skinned and crushed
350 g/12 oz demerara or light muscovado sugar
2 level tsp ground paprika
1 level tsp ground mixed spice
pinch of cayenne pepper
1 level tbsp salt
300 ml/½ pt distilled vinegar
225 g/8 oz seedless raisins

Place the tomatoes, onion and garlic in a saucepan and cook gently, uncovered, until a thick purée is obtained. Add sugar, paprika, mixed spice, cayenne, salt, vinegar and raisins.

Heat gently, stirring continuously until the sugar has dissolved. Increase the heat slightly and simmer, uncovered, stirring from time to time until the liquid is reduced – about 1 hour.

Pour into hot jars and seal with vinegar-proof tops and label.

Apple and Mint Chutney

MAKES ABOUT 1.8 KG/4 LB

*1.8 kg/4 lb cooking apples, peeled,
cored and chopped*
2 onions, skinned and chopped
450 g/1 lb sugar
1.1 ltr/2 pt malt vinegar
450 g/1 lb seedless raisins
25 g/1 oz root ginger, bruised
3 whole allspice
1 tsp salt
¼ level tsp cayenne pepper
6 level tbsp chopped fresh mint leaves

Place apples, onions, sugar, vinegar and raisins in a large saucepan. Tie root ginger and allspice in a muslin bag, and add to saucepan with the salt and cayenne pepper.

Heat gently, stirring continuously until sugar has dissolved. Increase the heat and simmer gently, uncovered, stirring from time to time to avoid sticking, until the mixture is thick and well reduced – about 45 minutes.

Discard the muslin bag and stir in the chopped mint; mix well.

Pour into hot jars and seal with vinegar-proof lids. Label.

Elderberry and Apple Chutney

MAKES ABOUT 1.4 KG/3 LB

*1.4 kg/3 lb cooking apples, peeled,
cored and sliced*
450 g/1 lb elderberries, stalks removed
*450 g/1 lb onions, skinned and
finely chopped*
700 g/1½ lb light muscovado sugar
900 ml/1½ pt malt vinegar
½ tsp salt
1 level tbsp mustard seeds
12 whole allspice
3 small pieces root ginger, bruised
1 level tsp black peppercorns

Place apples, elderberries, onion, sugar, vinegar and salt in a large saucepan. Tie the mustard seeds, whole allspice, ginger and peppercorns together in a muslin bag. Add these to the saucepan and bring slowly to the boil, stirring continuously, until the sugar has dissolved.

Simmer uncovered, stirring from time to time, until ingredients are soft and the contents of the pan are well reduced – about 1½ hours. Remove the muslin bag and press the bag through a coarse nylon sieve.

Pour into hot jars and cover with vinegar-proof lids. Label.

Red Plum Chutney

MAKES ABOUT 1.4 KG/3 LB

900 g/2 lb red plums, halved and stoned
*450 g/1 lb cooking apples, peeled,
cored and chopped*
450 g/1 lb onions, skinned and chopped
12 peppercorns
225 g/8 oz seedless raisins
*225 g/8 oz demerara or light
muscovado sugar*
2 level tsp ground ginger
1 level tsp ground mixed spice
2 tsp salt
½ tsp cayenne pepper
600 ml/1 pt pickling malt vinegar

Place the plums, apples and onions in a large saucepan. Tie the peppercorns in a muslin bag. Add to the saucepan with the remaining ingredients.

Bring slowly to the boil, stirring continuously, until the sugar has dissolved. Increase the heat and simmer uncovered until the chutney is thick and mushy – about 1¼ hours. Remove the muslin bag.

Fill the jars and seal with vinegar-proof tops. Label.

Crazy Orange and Rhubarb Chutney

MAKES ABOUT 1.8 KG/4 LB

2 oranges, scrubbed
1.1 kg/2½ lb prepared rhubarb
2 onions, skinned and chopped
900 g/2 lb demerara sugar
450 g/1 lb seedless raisins
900 ml/1½ pt malt vinegar
1 level tbsp mustard seeds
12 peppercorns
1 level tsp ground allspice

Grate the rind from the oranges on a fine grater. Squeeze the oranges to extract the juice and scoop the pulp into a bowl. Cut the rhubarb into 2.5 cm/1 in pieces and add to the orange with the onion, sugar, raisins and vinegar. Put into a large saucepan with the juice.

Tie the mustard seeds and peppercorns in a muslin bag. Put in the pan with the allspice and bring slowly to the boil, stirring continuously until the sugar has dissolved.

Simmer gently uncovered until thick and pulpy – about 1¾ hours.

Remove the muslin bag, pour into warm jars and seal with vinegar-proof tops. Label.

Sweet Pickled Orange and Lemon Rings

MAKES ABOUT 1.4 KG/3 LB

3 thin-skinned oranges, scrubbed
3 thin-skinned lemons, scrubbed
900 ml/1½ pt distilled vinegar
700 g/1½ lb golden granulated sugar
4 level tsp ground cloves
7 cm/3 in cinnamon stick
6 whole cloves

Slice the oranges and lemons into rounds 5 mm/¼ in thick. Put into a large saucepan with just enough water to cover and simmer gently until the rind is really soft – about 45 minutes.

Remove the fruit with a slotted spoon. Add vinegar, sugar, ground cloves and cinnamon to the juice in the pan. Bring to the boil and simmer gently for 10 minutes.

Return fruit to pan and cook gently until rind is transparent. With the slotted spoon, lift the fruit out of the syrup and pack into preheated jars. Go on boiling the syrup uncovered, until it begins to thicken – about 15 minutes.

Leave to cool, strain and pour over fruit. Add a few whole cloves to each jar. Cover and seal with vinegar-proof tops. Label.

Mango and Tomato Chutney

MAKES ABOUT 3.2 KG/7 LB

1.4 kg/3 lb unripe mangoes
450 g/1 lb onions, finely chopped
250 g/9 oz raisins
3 cloves garlic, crushed
4 yellow peppers, seeded and chopped
2 tbsp fresh root ginger, finely chopped
1 tsp ground allspice
700 g/1½ lb tomatoes, peeled and chopped
1 tbsp salt
700 ml/1¼ pt malt vinegar
800 g/1¾ lb light muscovado sugar

Peel the mangoes and cut the flesh from the stones. Chop and place in a preserving pan with the onion, raisins, garlic, peppers, ginger, allspice, tomatoes, salt and malt vinegar. Bring to the boil, cover and simmer for 30 minutes. Stir in the sugar and simmer, uncovered, for about 1 hour until thick. Stir from time to time.

Pour into clean, hot jars and seal with vinegar-proof tops. Cover and label.

Hot Mango Chutney

MAKES ABOUT 900 G/2 LB

*1 kg/2¼ lb mangoes (2 large), peeled,
halved and stoned*
50 g/2 oz salt
1.5 ltr/2½ pt water
350 g/12 oz granulated sugar
600 ml/1 pt spiced vinegar
*50 g/2 oz root ginger, peeled and
finely chopped*
4 cloves garlic, finely chopped
1 tsp chilli powder
1 green chilli, deseeded and chopped
50 g/2 oz raisins
50 g/2 oz dried dates, chopped
25 g/1 oz dried bananas (optional)
juice of 1 lemon
1 cinnamon stick

Cut the mangoes into small pieces and
place in a large bowl with the stones.
Sprinkle with salt and cover with water.
Allow to stand, covered with a plate or
film, for 24 hours.

Drain the mangoes in a plastic
colander or sieve and remove the
stones.

Pour the sugar and vinegar into a
preserving pan or a heavy-bottomed
saucepan. Allow the sugar to dissolve
over a low heat, stirring from time to
time then bring to the boil.

Add all the other ingredients and mix
well, bring back to the boil and simmer,
stirring frequently, until the chutney is
thick, about 30 minutes. Remove the
cinnamon.

Pour into hot jars, cover and label.
Allow to mature for at least a month.

Apple, Apricot or Pumpkin Chutney

MAKES 2 KG/4½ LB

*1 kg/2¼ lb apples or pumpkin, peeled,
cored or seeded and chopped or
450 g/1 lb dried apricots*
450 g/1 lb onions
225 g/8 oz seedless raisins
600 ml/1 pt white wine vinegar
450 g/1 lb dark muscovado sugar
225 g/8 oz preserved ginger
2 tsp mustard seeds
1 level tsp cayenne (optional)
salt
1 tsp ground turmeric
grated zest and juice of 1 orange
100 g/4 oz shelled walnuts

Put all the ingredients except the
walnuts into a pan and cook gently,
stirring over a low heat until the sugar is
dissolved. Bring up to the boil then
lower the heat and cook until a mushy
consistency (about 1½ hours).

Stir the walnuts into the mixture. Pack
into hot jars and seal. Label. Store for at
least a month before using.

Chunky Vegetable Pickle

MAKES ABOUT 1.4 KG/3 LB

225 g/8 oz carrots, scraped
225 g/8 oz swede, peeled
450 g/1 lb cooking apples, peeled and cored
1 large onion
225 g/8 oz small cauliflower florets
125 g/4 oz sultanas
200 g/7 oz muscovado sugar
3 level tbsp tomato purée
2 tbsp lemon juice
1 clove garlic, skinned and crushed
600 ml/1 pt malt vinegar
salt and milled pepper
½ level tsp ground mixed spice

Dice the carrots, swede and apple; chop
the onion. Blanch the carrots in boiling,
salted water for 4 minutes, drain well.

Place the carrots with all other
ingredients in a large saucepan. Bring
slowly to the boil, stirring continuously
until the sugar has dissolved. Increase
heat and simmer uncovered until
vegetables are just tender and contents
of pan are well reduced – about 1¼
hours.

Pour into hot jars and seal with
vinegar-proof tops. Label.

CHAPTER SEVEN

Flavoured Vinegars and Oils

~

MANY VARIETIES OF herb-flavoured and spiced oils and vinegars are available in the supermarkets. These will enhance salad dressings, homemade chutneys and pickles. However, if you have herbs in the garden or the window box, you will find it easy to make your own inexpensively. Flavoured oils and vinegars make excellent and welcome gifts, so make some extra to give to friends. Save any interesting bottles to store them.

VINEGAR

For more subtle flavours, use wine or cider vinegar to make dressings, although strong malt vinegar may be used for pickling. Try to buy large containers of vinegar or oil to make flavoured products, as small bottles from the supermarket are less cost-effective.

Vinegar-proof seals are essential for bottles and jars. Use new corks or waxed paper to seal and clingfilm is useful if the product is cold when sealed.

The best vinegar should be used for pickling and it should have an acetic acid content of at least 5%. Distilled vinegar, which is colourless, gives a good appearance but malt vinegar may give a better flavour to pickles. Cider vinegar is excellent for some chutneys and fruit pickles.

There is some difference of opinion as to whether the vinegar is best used hot or cold. Try both methods and decide which is the best. One school of thought says that the vinegar has to be boiled with some herbs or it becomes sour. Others feel that the vinegar keeps fairly well whatever is pickled in it. A good rule of thumb is that cold vinegar is best for pickling vegetables which need to be kept crisp, e.g. onions and red cabbage. Hot vinegar is better with the softer type of pickles such as plums and walnuts.

Herb vinegars

These are easy to make and add extra flavour to dressings and marinades. Gather the herbs preferably just before they flower but you can use the fresh herbs available in the supermarkets if you do not grow your own.

Floral vinegars

These are made in the same way as the herb variety and they can be used in fruit salads and cosmetic recipes. Again fresh flowers from the garden are best; choose from elderflowers, nasturtiums, lavender, clover, rose petals, rosemary flowers, thyme flowers and sweet violets. Remove the stems and any green or white parts from the petals.

Fruit vinegars

These are mostly made from soft fruits such as raspberries and blackberries and were much used to ease sore throats in great-grandmother's time. Today they make an excellent addition to a plain steamed pudding or batter and have come back into fashion for dressings and marinades.

OILS

Use a good quality olive, safflower or sunflower oil. However, beware of using any oil with a strong flavour. It is much cheaper to make your own flavoured oils and a good range will enhance the flavour of your meat, fish and vegetable cooking as well as salad dressings. Basil or garlic oil, for example, will flavour pizzas as well as tomato dishes, hot or cold.

To make chilli oil, pour oil into a bottle containing dried or fresh chillies. Keep for four weeks.

To make a sweet oil use almond oil with scented flowers such as lavender, pinks, rose petals and lemon verbena.

Herbal Vinegar

Use bay leaves, basil, chervil, dill, fennel, lemon balm, marjoram, mint, rosemary, summer savory, tarragon or thyme.

MAKES 600 ML/1 PT

600 ml/1 pt cider or white wine vinegar
fresh herbs

Bruise the fresh herbs with the back of a spoon or a weight covered in clingfilm. Put into a clean jar.

Heat the vinegar but do not boil and pour over the herbs when it is warm. Seal with a vinegar-proof top and place on a warm sunny window ledge. Lift the bottle or jar and shake every day for at least two weeks.

Strain the vinegar and taste for flavour. If a stronger herb taste is required, put more fresh herbs in the vinegar and repeat the process.

Strain into a clean bottle or jar and add a sprig of fresh herb for decoration and identification.

Spiced Vinegar

Use whole spices as the ground variety gives a cloudy result.

MAKES 1.1 LTR/2 PT

1.1 ltr/2 pt malt vinegar
1 cinnamon stick
½ tsp whole cloves
½ tsp whole mace
½ tsp whole allspice

Pour the cold vinegar into a sterilized jar or bottle and put the spices into the vinegar. Shake well and seal with a vinegar-proof top. Keep in a cool place for one or two months, taking the container out and shaking every week.

Strain into a suitable sterilized container and use as required for pickles and chutneys.

Tarragon Vinegar

MAKES ABOUT 600 ML/1 PT

freshly gathered tarragon leaves, washed
600 ml/1 pt white wine vinegar

Use a wide-mouthed jar which will hold just over the 600 ml/1 pt, or adjust the quantity of vinegar.

Preferably use the herbs just before the plants flower and half fill the jar with the leaves then pour on the vinegar. Put on a vinegar-proof stopper and shake well. Allow the vinegar to steep for at least two weeks, though five weeks is better.

Use as required without straining.

Aromatic Rosemary Vinegar

MAKES 600 ML/1 PT

600 ml/1 pt white wine vinegar
several large sprigs of rosemary, washed

Put the cold vinegar in a suitable bottle and feed in the branches of the rosemary. Leave the bottle, suitably stoppered, for about four to six weeks before using.

Strain and put a small sprig of fresh rosemary into the bottle for identification.

Hot Spiced Vinegar

Use whole spices for this recipe.

MAKES 4.5 LTR/8 PT

4.5 ltr/8 pt malt vinegar
350 g/12 oz sugar
3 cloves garlic, lightly crushed
15 g/1/2 oz allspice
15 g/1/2 oz mace
15 g/1/2 oz celery seed
15 g/1/2 oz cloves
15 g/1/2 oz mustard seed
15 g/1/2 oz peppercorns
15 g/1/2 oz root ginger
1 tsp coriander seeds

Put all the ingredients in a large pan and bring to the boil slowly. Allow to boil for about 5 minutes then cover and allow to cool naturally. Pour into containers with the spices and allow to stand for four weeks. The spices can be strained off or left, as liked.

Mint Vinegar

MAKES 600 ML/1 PT

600 ml/1 pt white wine vinegar
large bunch of mint, washed
1 tsp caster sugar

Heat the vinegar in a saucepan. Crush half the mint leaves into the pan with the vinegar, add the sugar and bring the vinegar to the boil. Remove immediately from the heat and allow to become cold.

Place the remaining mint leaves in a bottle and strain in the cooled vinegar. The vinegar is ready to use but the flavour will become stronger with time.

Garlic Vinegar

MAKES 600 ML/1 PT

600 ml/1 pt red or white wine vinegar
6 cloves garlic

Put the vinegar into a clean jar or a bottle. Slice 3 cloves of garlic and put into the vinegar, stopper the top and place on a sunny window ledge for about 14 days.

Shake the bottle daily then strain into a clean bottle, add the remaining cloves of garlic peeled but left whole, put on a lid or vinegar-proof stopper and use as required.

Chilli Vinegar

MAKES 600 ML/1 PT

600 ml/1 pt malt vinegar
25 g/1 oz dried red chillies

Bring the vinegar to the boil and put in the dried chillies. Pour into a jar or a bottle and keep for five or six weeks, turning over from time to time. Alternatively, boil up the vinegar and add 50 g/2 oz fresh chillies, deseeded and cut into halves. Both these vinegars are strong and you will only need a few drops for seasoning.

Chilli Sherry

This makes an excellent flavouring for oriental dishes. Put 6 fresh chillies in a bottle and pour in the sherry, stopper and keep for 2 weeks before using. The bottle can be topped up with sherry as it is used.

Sherry Ginger is a successful way to store excess fresh root ginger as this goes mouldy quite quickly in the refrigerator and vegetable rack. Peel the ginger, place in a suitable small jar and cover with sherry. Delicious for flavouring oriental dishes or ginger-flavoured puddings.

Raspberry Vinegar

This can also be made with blackcurrants and blackberries.

MAKES 1 LTR/1¾ PT

450 g/1 lb ripe raspberries, hulled and washed
600 ml/1 pt malt vinegar
sugar

Put the raspberries into a bowl with the vinegar and cover with a cloth or film and leave to stand for five days, stirring occasionally.

Strain and measure the liquid into a pan and for each 600 ml/1 pt liquid add 450 g/1 lb sugar. Bring to the boil for 10 minutes and bottle.

Fragrant Herbal Oils

Use basil, chervil, dill, fennel, lemon balm, marjoram, mint, rosemary, summer savory, tarragon, thyme or garlic.

MAKES 600 ML/1 PT

600 ml/1 pt good quality oil
fresh herbs

Bruise the fresh herbs with the back of a spoon or a weight covered in film. Put into a clean jar and cover with unheated oil. Put on a lid and allow to stand on a sunny window ledge for about two weeks.

Strain the oil through a sieve lined with muslin. If a stronger herb taste is required use more fresh herbs in the oil and repeat the process.

Strain into a clean bottle or jar and add a sprig of the fresh herb for decoration and identification.

CHAPTER EIGHT

Home
Pickling

~

ALTHOUGH THERE ARE many excellent pickles produced commercially I have noticed that many more people are now making their own.

Use good quality young vegetables, wash and remove outer leaves or any blemishes. These can be soaked in brine or sprinkled with salt in layers as preferred. To make brine, add 450 g/1 lb water. Rinse the salt from the vegetables and drain before pickling in the vinegar or they will be too salty.

Pack the vegetables in sterilized jars and allow 1 cm/½ in of vinegar at the top of the jar. There will be some evaporation and if the vegetables are left uncovered they will become discoloured.

After the vinegar has been poured in the jars they should be covered tightly with vinegar-proof tops. Waxed paper tied with string is suitable or use clingfilm for sealing cold pickles. Beware of using metal caps as they are likely to react with the vinegar.

Garlicky Pickled Cucumbers

MAKES 1 KG/2¼ LB

*1 kg/2¼ lb small cucumbers
(8–12 cm/3–5 in long)
225 g/8 oz cooking salt
2.4 ltr/4 pt water
Spiced Vinegar (see page 68)
2 cloves garlic, peeled and sliced*

Scrub the cucumbers and rinse well, lay them in a glass or china bowl. Pour on the salt and then the water and stir round. Cover with clingfilm and leave for three days.

Pack the cucumbers into sterilized jars, either whole or cut into rings.

Heat the spiced vinegar with the garlic and pour over the cucumbers. Cover with clingfilm and leave for 24 hours in a warm kitchen or airing cupboard.

Drain off the vinegar and boil up again (you may need to add more), pour over the cucumbers and leave for another 24 hours. Repeat the process until the cucumbers have become darker.

Seal with vinegar-proof tops and allow to stand for at least one week before using.

If liked, put a sprig of dill and some dill flowers in each jar in the final stage before storing.

Pickled Red Cabbage

MAKES ABOUT 1.8 KG/4 LB

*1 red cabbage
cooking salt
Spiced Vinegar (see page 68)*

Remove any discoloured leaves from the outside of the cabbage and shred finely (this can be done in the food processor). Arrange a layer of cabbage and sprinkle with salt, continue with another layer of cabbage and salt until the final layer is salted. Allow to stand for 24 hours.

Wash and rinse the cabbage to remove excess salt. Pack into jars (the amount will depend on the size of the cabbage) and cover with spiced vinegar. Eat after three or four days for a crisp pickle. Although the cabbage will keep for several months it will become soft after about 2 months.

Pickled Walnuts

The walnuts must be picked around the end of June before they become woody and develop a shell. They can be tested by pricking with a needle and if any shell is felt the nut should be discarded for this purpose. Beware of the stain; it is better to use disposable plastic gloves for this task.

MAKES QUANTITY OF NUTS PREPARED

Walnuts as available
450 g/1 lb salt
4.5 ltr/8 pt water
1.75 ltr/3 pt malt vinegar
450 g/1 lb dark muscovado sugar
1½ tsp salt
1 tsp whole mixed spice
1 tsp black peppercorns
½ tsp cloves

Make up half the salt and water and cover the nuts in a glass or china bowl for three or four days. Drain the nuts and steep in the other half of the brine solution for one week.

Drain the nuts and arrange on plastic trays or china dishes and leave the nuts for about one day until they have turned completely black. Put the remaining ingredients in a saucepan and dissolve the sugar slowly. Bring to the boil for about 5 minutes. Allow to cool for several hours then strain out the spices.

Arrange the walnuts in jars, heat up the strained vinegar and pour on to the walnuts. Cover the jars with vinegar-proof tops and allow to stand for at least four weeks before opening.

Pickled Horseradish

MAKES 225 G/8 OZ

Horseradish roots, washed and grated
½ tsp sugar for each jar
½ tsp salt for each jar
1 fresh chilli, sliced (optional)
white malt vinegar

Fill small sterilized jars two thirds full with grated horseradish. Add sugar and salt to each jar with a slice of chilli. Cover with vinegar and cover for storage.

Use for horseradish sauce for beef or smoked fish and for sprinkling on beetroot.

Pickled Onions

MAKES 1.8 KG/4 LB

1.8 kg/4 lb pickling onions
450 g/1 lb salt
4.5 ltr/8 pt water
Spiced Vinegar (see page 68)

Use small even-sized onions and put them in a large basin or pot with the skins on. Make up half the salt and water into a brine and pour over the onions. Leave the onions for 12 hours then drain, peel and return to the basin. Make up the other half of the brine and pour over the peeled onions. Allow to stand for at least 36 hours. Use a plate or lid to keep the onions under the brine.

Drain the onions in a plastic colander or sieve thoroughly and then pack into sterilized jars. Pour on the cold spiced vinegar, seal and store for at least three or four months before using.

Pickled Mushrooms

MAKES 450 G/1 LB

450 g/1 lb button mushrooms, washed
600 ml/1 pt Spiced Vinegar (see page 68)
2 blades mace
½ tsp white pepper
1 tsp salt
1 tsp ground ginger
½ onion

Put the mushrooms in a pan with 300 ml/½ pt vinegar, add the other ingredients and cook on a low heat until the mushrooms become smaller and cooked. Strain the mushrooms and pack into sterilized jars.

Add the remaining 300 ml/½ pt vinegar to the pan and reheat. When hot pour on to the mushrooms. Seal and cover.

Green Tomato Pickle

MAKES ABOUT 1.4 KG/3 LB

1.4 kg/3 lb green tomatoes, washed
salt
300 ml/½ pt vinegar
1 tsp ground cinnamon

Use 15 g/½ oz salt to 1 ltr/1¾ pt water and boil the tomatoes for about 10 minutes. Lift out with a fork and peel off the skin. Boil the vinegar, cinnamon and 150 ml/¼ pt water together, add the tomatoes and boil for 5 minutes. Pour into a plastic or glass bowl, cover with film and allow to stand for a week.

Strain off the vinegar and boil in a pan for 10 minutes, add the tomatoes and cook for 5 minutes. Pack into sterilized jars and seal while hot.

Spiced Mixed Vegetable Pickle

MAKES ABOUT 1.8 KG/4 LB

1 cauliflower, cut into small florets
450 g/1 lb pickling onions, peeled and halved
450 g/1 lb French beans, trimmed and sliced
2 small cucumbers, washed and cut into rounds
225 g/8 oz cooking salt
2.4 ltr/4 pt water
Spiced Vinegar (see page 68)

Prepare the vegetables and put into a large glass or china basin. Sprinkle over the salt and pour on the water, mix well and cover with film and leave to stand for at least 48 hours.

Wash and drain the vegetables and pack into jars, leaving some space for the vinegar to surround the vegetables. Cover with the cold spiced vinegar and seal with vinegar-proof lids. Allow to stand for at least two weeks before using.

Hot Piccalilli

There are two main types of piccalilli, the hot variety and the sweeter pickle.

MAKES 2.8 KG/6 LB

450 g/1 lb salt
4.5 ltr/8 pt water
2.8 kg/6 lb mixed fresh vegetables
(cauliflower florets, pickling onions or shallots, green beans, marrow, strips of pepper, diced cucumber)
15 g/$\frac{1}{2}$ oz turmeric
30 g/1$\frac{1}{4}$ oz dry mustard
30 g/1$\frac{1}{4}$ oz ground ginger
175 g/6 oz sugar
1 tbsp cornflour
1.1 ltr/2 pt white vinegar

Make up the salt and water in a large basin and as the vegetables are prepared drop them into the brine. Cover with a heavy lid, plate or board to keep the vegetables immersed in the brine. Allow the vegetables to soak in the brine for 24 hours before rinsing in cold water and draining.

Measure the spices with the sugar into a large pan. Add three quarters of the vinegar and stir on a low heat until well mixed and the sugar is dissolved.

Add the prepared vegetables and stir until well coated with the spice mixture and the vegetables are slightly tender. However, they are better crisp (not hard) but should not be overcooked.

Lift the vegetables out with a slotted spoon and pack into sterilized jars, allowing enough space for the sauce.

Mix the cornflour with the remaining vinegar and mix into the liquid in the pan. Boil for a few minutes. Pour the sauce into the jars, turning around to allow it to coat the vegetables. Alternatively, you can thicken the sauce while the vegetables are still in the pan, making sure that no lumps form, and then pack into jars.

Sweet Piccalilli

MAKES 2.8 KG/6 LB

450 g/1 lb salt
4.5 ltr/8 pt water
2.8 kg/6 lb mixed fresh vegetables
(cauliflower florets, pickling onions or shallots, green beans, marrow, strips of pepper, diced cucumber, green tomatoes and sliced celery)
15 g/$\frac{1}{2}$ oz turmeric
20 g/$\frac{3}{4}$ oz dry mustard
1$\frac{1}{2}$ tsp ground ginger
250 g/8 oz sugar
2 tbsp cornflour
1.75 ltr/3 pt white vinegar

Make up the salt and water in a large basin and as the vegetables are prepared drop them into the brine. Cover with a heavy lid, plate or board to keep the vegetables immersed in the brine. Allow the vegetables to soak in the brine for 24 hours before rinsing in cold water and draining.

Measure the spices with the sugar into a large pan. Add three quarters of the vinegar and stir round over a low heat until well mixed and the sugar is dissolved.

Add the prepared vegetables and stir until well coated with the spice mixture and the vegetables are slightly tender. However, they are better crisp (not hard) and on no account should be overcooked until soft and mushy.

Lift the vegetables out with a slotted spoon and pack into sterilized jars, allowing enough space for the sauce to go around them.

Mix the cornflour with the remaining vinegar and mix into the liquid in the pan. Boil for a few minutes. Pour the sauce into the jars, turning around to allow it to coat the vegetables.

CHAPTER NINE

Crystallized,
Candied and
Glacé Fruits

~

THESE ARE EXPENSIVE to buy and often imported from France. The fruits take a long time to prepare, but it is easy and much cheaper to prepare candied fruits at home if you have the time and patience. The process consists of covering the fruit at first with a light, hot syrup, made with granulated sugar, and then continuing the process over several days with increased sugar syrup until the fruit is totally impregnated with sugar. The fruit is often finished by crystallizing which gives it a sugary appearance, or by glazing in a syrup, which gives a glacé finish.

SUITABLE FRUIT AND PEEL

Apricots, cherries, pineapples, plums, peaches and grapes are all suitable. Peel of citrus fruits and angelica can also be treated but flower petals and herb leaves need a different process (see later).

It is best to candy each fruit separately to retain the individual flavours. Small fruits, such as cherries and apricots, should be stoned and larger fruits peeled and halved. Fruit should be fresh and firm. Soft fruits such as raspberries and strawberries are not suitable.

CANDIED FRUIT

This process can take two weeks for larger pieces of fruit.

Preparation

Whole fruit should be pricked by a fork (all old cook books stipulate a silver fork but a stainless steel one will serve); larger fruits can be halved or quartered.

Prepare the fruit and then weigh it before putting it in a large saucepan, cover with hot water and simmer until just soft but not overcooked or mushy. Reserve the cooking liquid and transfer the fruit into a large heatproof bowl large enough to keep the fruit covered.

For every 450 g/1 lb prepared fruit a syrup will be needed, which can be made up with the cooking liquid to 300 ml/½ pt. To the water add 50 g/2 oz sugar and 100 g/4 oz glucose (all sugar can be used, but this mixture is better).

Bring the sugar and water slowly to the boil to allow the sugar to dissolve and continue boiling until you have a thin syrup. If there is not enough, make more as the fruit must be covered.

Method

1 Pour the hot syrup over the fruit until completely covered. Place clingfilm over the top of the bowl and leave for 24 hours.

2 Drain off the syrup into a saucepan and add 50 g/2 oz sugar. Bring to the boil and pour over the fruit again. Repeat this process of adding the extra sugar, boiling the syrup and pouring over the fruit for four more days.

3 On the fifth day drain off the syrup into a saucepan and add 75 g/3 oz sugar or glucose to the syrup. Add the fruit from the bowl and boil for 3 minutes. Return the fruit and syrup to the bowl and allow to stand covered for 48 hours.

4 Repeat stage 3 and then leave the fruit to soak for four days. By now the syrup should be very thick, almost like honey. If the syrup is not as thick as this repeat stage 3 again.

Drying

Arrange a wire tray over a clean plastic tray or dish and lift the fruit from the syrup with a slotted spoon on to the wire tray. After it has dripped it can be left to dry in a warm airing cupboard or kitchen. The temperature should not be more than 50°C/120°F. If the temperature is steady the fruits will dry out in a few hours, otherwise it might take some days. Turn the fruit from time to time until it is completely dry and then it is ready to use.

CRYSTALLIZED FRUIT

To finish the fruit in this way, have ready a layer of granulated sugar on paper laid out on a tray. Dip each fruit into boiling water and drain off excess moisture. Roll each fruit in the sugar until coated, and allow to dry.

GLACÉ FRUITS

Make these in a warm dry atmosphere or the fruits may remain sticky.

1 Make a new syrup of 450 g/1 lb sugar slowly dissolved in 150 ml/¼ pt water, then brought to the boil. Keep the syrup in a tightly covered dish.

2 Heat a dish or cup by pouring boiling water on to it and then emptying. Pour a small amount of syrup into the warm dish or cup.

3 Dip the candied fruit in boiling water and drain. Dip into the syrup in the cup and arrange on a wire tray. When the syrup in the cup becomes cloudy discard the syrup and replace with more.

4 When all the fruits are arranged on the wire tray allow to dry in a warm dry atmosphere, turning over from time to time.

Marrons Glacés

These are not the same as the commercially prepared chestnuts from France as it is impossible to produce those at home. However, these are delicious to eat and worth doing when chestnuts are in season.

---

1 kg/2¼ lb chestnuts
450 g/1 lb sugar
450 g/1 lb glucose
300 ml/½ pt water (for syrup)
vanilla essence

Remove the shells by making a slit at the pointed end of each nut with a sharp knife. Place them in a large saucepan and cover with cold water. Bring the water slowly to the boil and cook for 2 minutes. Remove from the water with a slotted spoon and take off the shells when cool enough to handle (use rubber gloves).

To prepare in the microwave make the slits at the ends and microwave on full power for 3 minutes for each 225 g/8 oz, turn the chestnuts after 2 minutes, then turn out and peel.

Put the peeled chestnuts into a pan, cover with cold water, bring gently to the boil and simmer until tender. Drain carefully to avoid breaking.

While the chestnuts are cooking make a syrup in a large pan by mixing the sugar and glucose with the water over a low heat and stir until the sugar is dissolved. Bring to the boil for about 4 minutes, then add the chestnuts and gently bring the pan back to the boil. Cover the pan and allow to stand overnight in a warm place.

Bring the saucepan back to the boil, cover and allow to stand for a further 24 hours. Add a few drops of vanilla essence and slowly bring to the boil again.

Allow the syrup to cool slightly, then remove the chestnuts from the syrup and drain on a wire cooling rack placed over a tray to catch the drips. Use the glacé method to finish.

Candied Angelica

Use the stalks of the plant when young and tender, which means cutting them in April or May. Trim off the roots and leaf end and place the stalks in a basin.

Make a brine by putting 2 tbsp salt into 1.1 ltr/2 pt water. Bring to the boil and pour over the stalks and allow to soak for about 10 minutes. Drain and rinse in cold water, then put in a saucepan of boiling water. Boil for 5 minutes or longer if the stalks seem tough. Scrape the stalks to remove the outer skin.

Make a syrup of 225 g/8 oz sugar and 225 g/8 oz glucose dissolved slowly in 600 ml/1 pt water. Boil until the liquid becomes slightly thicker.

Arrange the angelica in a long plastic box. Pour the syrup on top of the angelica and leave for about two weeks, topping up with glucose every second day until the syrup is thick.

Candied Peel

Prepare the skins of oranges, grapefruit and lemons by scrubbing the skins thoroughly. Cut in half and remove the juice and pulp.

Boil the skins for about 1 hour, changing the water several times. Drain and follow the procedure for angelica, allowing the peel to soak for three weeks. Finish as for Glacé Fruits.

Use the left-over syrup for fruit salads or stewing fruits or dilute and use for any further candying process again.

Crystallized Flowers

These can be made at home and make lovely decorations for cakes and desserts.

Use almost any flower except those grown from bulbs as those are poisonous or indeed any poisonous plants. Small flowers such as violets, primroses and cherry blossoms are most suitable. Pick on a dry day without rain or dew on the petals.

Gum arabic and rose water are both available from chemists.

Method 1

Pour 2 tbsp rose water into a screw-top jar with 15 g/½ oz gum arabic. Shake well and put to one side for several hours, shaking the jar every 30 minutes.

Line a baking sheet with parchment paper. Cut the stalks from the flowers, or leave small stalks if using tiny sprigs. Individual petals can also be removed from the heads.

Use a small, soft paintbrush and brush both sides of the flowers with the gum arabic mixture. Dip the flowers into caster sugar and place on the baking sheet. Leave in a warm place to dry. Store in a glass jar with an airtight lid.

Method 2

Make a syrup using 450 g/1 lb sugar and a scant 300 ml/½ pt water. Simmer until the sugar is dissolved and then boil for about 5–7 minutes.

Drop the petals or flower heads into the syrup and boil for 1 minute. Remove from the syrup with a slotted spoon, drain and arrange on a tray lined with waxed paper. Use tweezers to arrange the petals if necessary.

Leave in a warm place for 24 hours to dry. Store in an airtight glass jar.

Index